Emerson's Rhetoric of Revelation

Emerson's Rhetoric of Revelation

Nature, the Reader, and
the Apocalypse Within

Alan D. Hodder

The Pennsylvania State University Press
University Park and London

Passages from Emerson's *Collected Works, The Journals and Miscellaneous Notebooks,* and *Early Lectures* reprinted by permission of Harvard University Press.

Selections from *Young Emerson Speaks: Unpublished Discourses on Many Subjects* by Ralph Waldo Emerson, edited by Arthur Cushman McGiffert, Jr. Copyright 1935 by the Ralph Waldo Emerson Memorial Association. Copyright renewed 1966 by Arthur Cushman McGiffert, Jr., and The Ralph Waldo Emerson Memorial Association. Reprinted by permission of Houghton Mifflin Company.

Excerpt from "Little Gidding" in *Four Quartets,* copyright 1943 by T. S. Eliot; renewed 1971 by Esme Valerie Eliot. Reprinted by permission of Harcourt Brace Jovanovich, Inc.

Library of Congress Cataloging-in-Publication Data

Hodder, Alan D.
   Emerson's rhetoric of revelation : Nature, the reader, and the
apocalypse within / Alan D. Hodder.

     p. cm.
   Bibliography: p.
   Includes index.
   ISBN 0-271-00643-9
   1. Emerson, Ralph Waldo, 1803–1882. Nature. 2. Reader-response
criticism. 3. Apocalyptic literature—History and criticism.
I. Title.
PS1613.H64 1989
814'.3—dc19   88-10925
                                                  CIP

To my teachers

And I saw a new heaven and a new earth; for the first heaven and the first earth were passed away. . . .

—Revelation 21.1

It would give scope for many truths in experimental religion to preach from the text of 'There shall be new heavens and a new earth.'

—Emerson, 1834

. . . art has two constant, two unending concerns: it always meditates on death and thus always creates life. All great, genuine art resembles and continues the Revelation of St. John.

—Boris Pasternak

Contents

Preface

In bringing this study into critical resolution, I have benefited enormously, as the following pages will show, from the vast and frequently incisive secondary literature which has grown up around Emerson and *Nature*, but especially the work of such critics as Joel Porte, Barbara Packer, Harold Bloom, and Julie Ellison; yet I hope that even these writers will discover something here which they have not seen before. I have tried in this representation of *Nature* and its long foreground to articulate what seems essential about Emerson's first book and by implication distinctive of his contribution to American letters generally. The result, I think, is a revision of certain common assumptions about *Nature* and a fuller recovery of its specifically religious dimensions and affiliations. I naturally hope that Emerson scholars and other students of American literature will find this book useful, but I also hope that it will prove edifying to those concerned with the multifaceted relationship between religion and literature generally, whatever their particular level of expertise or field of interest.

With books, archives, and faculty no university is as richly endowed for research on Emerson as Harvard, and I have been fortunate to have access to such extensive resources. In the early years of my work, I received expert guidance from several members of the faculty at Harvard and elsewhere without whom the path to this book would have been considerably more roundabout than it has been. I would like to thank Andy Delbanco for helping to initiate me into American studies at Harvard, and for his generous support and wise, if at times sobering, counsel. I would like to acknowledge my indebtedness to Richard R. Niebuhr for his exact and illuminating discourses on Coleridge and for the assurance which resulted from his careful early reading of my manuscript. I would also like to register my thanks to Phyllis Cole, whose discussions of Mary Moody Emerson helped clarify my intuitions at an early stage in my thinking about the significance of Emerson's relationship with his favorite aunt. And I would like to thank Joel Myerson for his expert and meticulous reading of my manuscript at a later stage in its development, and for his several recommendations which I have sought to incorporate here.

The three academic counselors to whom I owe the largest debt of gratitude, however, are James Engell, Joel Porte, and Warner Berthoff. As both colleague and advisor, Jim Engell has helped me unstintingly and generously over the past several years, and his informed reading of my manuscript at several stages in its development has helped to improve it in several indispensable respects. Special thanks go also to Joel Porte, whose writing on Emerson provided the starting point for my study, as I will show, and whose teaching constituted for me a genuinely Emersonian provocation. I would especially like to express my deepest thanks to Warner Berthoff for his sustaining confidence in my work, for his erudition as a scholar, and for his example as a teacher of literature.

Finally, I would like to express my abiding gratitude to two persons whose contributions to this work run far deeper than its visible compass: first, my wife, Harbour Fraser Hodder, whose insights into poetry and the creative process have helped shape my ideas at so many points and on so many occasions that I no longer know which to call hers and which to call my own, and second, Maharishi Mahesh Yogi, whose teachings inform this treatment at several turns, and who first alerted me to the human significance of Bhagavad Gītā 9.8 and the personal value of easting.

Abbreviations

For convenience, the following abbreviations are used in the text to identify sources of material cited:

CEC   *The Correspondence of Emerson and Carlyle,* ed. Joseph Slater. New York and London: Columbia University Press, 1964.

CW   *The Collected Works of Ralph Waldo Emerson,* ed. Robert E. Spiller, Alfred R. Ferguson, Joseph Slater, and Jean Ferguson Carr. 4 vols. Cambridge: Harvard University Press, 1971, 1979, 1983, 1987.

EL   *The Early Lectures of Ralph Waldo Emerson,* ed. Stephen E. Whicher, Robert E. Spiller, and Wallace E. Williams. 3 vols. Cambridge: Harvard University Press, 1959, 1964, 1972.

J   *The Journals of Ralph Waldo Emerson,* ed. Edward Waldo Emerson and Waldo Emerson Forbes. 10 vols. Boston and New York: Houghton Mifflin, 1909–14.

JMN   *The Journals and Miscellaneous Notebooks of Ralph Waldo Emerson,* ed. William H. Gilman, Alfred R. Ferguson, George P. Clark, Merrell R. Davis, Merton M. Sealts, Harrison Hayford, Ralph H. Orth, J. E. Parsons, A. W. Plumstead, Linda Allardt, and Susan Sutton Smith. 16 vols. Cambridge: Harvard University Press, 1960–82.

L   *The Letters of Ralph Waldo Emerson,* ed. Ralph L. Rusk. 6 vols. New York and London: Columbia University Press, 1939.

W   *The Complete Works of Ralph Waldo Emerson,* Centenary Edition. 14 vols. Boston and New York: Houghton Mifflin, 1903–4.

YES   *Young Emerson Speaks: Unpublished Discourses on Many Subjects by Ralph Waldo Emerson,* ed. Arthur Cushman McGiffert, Jr. Boston: Houghton Mifflin, 1938.

Textual Notes:

When citing the Bible, I have kept to the usage of the Authorized King James Version. When quoting from JMN, I have for the most part omitted the textual apparatus for the sake of easier reading. Where in the few cases I have retained the apparatus of the Harvard text, I have done so for specific illustrative purposes.

Introduction

Forgetfulness turning to recall epitomizes the characteristic movement of *Nature*. Or at least so one might conclude after trying to
resolve the refractoriness, apparent inconsistency, and even con-
tradictoriness of Emerson's notoriously self-reliant sentences.
Sometimes it is hard to resist the thought that his favorite figure of
speech was actually the non sequitur, since the whole grand structure of his first book seems to rest on one. It speaks, for instance, of
"Nature," but deals mainly with Spirit. For the scrupulous reader,
the conclusion of *Nature* does not exactly follow. Francis Bowen,
reviewing Emerson's little book for *The Christian Examiner* in
1837, noted the "beautiful writing and sound philosophy" in the
early chapters, devoted as they were to the "uses of the material
world," but objected to the later ones, where, adopting a Berke-
leyan metaphysics, "the author turns and aims a back blow at the
universe, which he has been leading us to admire and love. The
heavens are rolled together like a scroll, the solid earth cracks
beneath our feet, . . . Matter," it turns out, "is nothing. Spirit is
all."[1]

There are several turns at which an attentive reader might fall
prey to *Nature*'s inveigling, but it is the title itself which has
proved the most misleading. From the time of its first appearance,
Nature has continually led its critics into the field looking for
clues to its origin and identity. Even so incisive a contemporary

critic as Barbara Packer looks to Emerson's fascination with light
and optics for the formula which explains *Nature*'s essential mysteries. *Nature,* she assumes, is Emerson's raid on nature, his
"crack with the sphinx."[2]

If the title does not throw a conscientious reader off the track,
the Introduction generally will. After the stirring oratory of the
first two paragraphs—culminating with the exhortations "Let us
interrogate the great apparition, that shines so peacefully around
us. Let us inquire, to what end is nature?"—*Nature*'s voice suddenly sobers down to the level of professorial cant: "All science
has one aim, namely, to find a theory of nature," and, "Philosophically considered, the universe is composed of Nature and the Soul.
Strictly speaking, therefore, all that is separate from us, all which
Philosophy distinguishes as the Not Me, that is, both nature and
art, all other men and my own body, must be ranked under this
name, Nature" (CW, I, 7–8).

Though we are lucky enough to escape this classroom atmosphere for periods of recess out of doors, we are dutifully ushered
back in toward the end of our investigations for a lecture on
"Idealism." The burden of this talk, so it seems, is to marshal
support for the "Ideal theory," which holds that "matter is a phenomenon, not substance," common sense notwithstanding, and
thus to suggest a solution to the problem of the apparent divorce
between Nature and Spirit. The character of this discussion is
unambiguous enough: its tone is academic. It conforms roughly to
canons of philosophical method; it is inductive and systematic; it
produces evidence weighing on the theory it proposes. Are we
then to be blamed for anticipating a sincere and consistent resolution of the problem, or at least an attempt? But the demonstration
leaves off in midstream, and Emerson cheerfully announces that
since his theory "does not satisfy the demands of the spirit," it can
only stand "as a useful introductory hypothesis." In all this apparent philosophizing, we have scarcely got beyond the main question when, in a cloud of smoke, we quit the schoolroom and descend into "the recesses of consciousness" (CW, I, 37–38).

It is true that in the weeks just prior to the publication of
Nature Emerson complained to his brother William of an unidenti-
fied "crack" in his book, "not easy to be soldered or welded," and

scholars may well be justified in surmising that this disjunction arose out of Emerson's own inability to arrive at a philosophically satisfying resolution of the ancient antinomy between Nature and Spirit. But what are we to make of the odd modulation of tone here, the blithe and carefree abandonment of the whole rational enterprise? Oliver Wendell Holmes facetiously characterized the language of *Nature* as that "of one who is just coming to himself after having been etherized," and this is just one juncture where Holmes's curious remark may shed unexpected light.[3]

If we did not know better, we might suspect the author of a premature weakness of attention, a kind of aphasia of the pen. There *is* a lapse here—an abandonment and a forgetting—but there is nothing absentminded about it. Emerson's lapses have the license of method. They are salutary and, we might say, saltatory. They aim to advance, not frustrate, the "argument." Nature, Emerson had already begun to realize, provides no answers: the solution to the Sphinx's riddle lies not with the Sphinx but with the Man: "Away profane philosopher! seekest thou in nature the cause? This refers to that, and that to the next, and the next to the third, and everything refers. Thou must ask in another mood, thou must feel it and love it, thou must behold it in a spirit as grand as that by which it exists, ere thou canst know the law" (CW, I, 125).

The clue provided in this oration on "The Method of Nature," delivered at Waterville College five years after the first publication of *Nature,* goes a long way to explain the fluctuations of voice and the apparent inconsistencies of Emerson's first and in many ways his most enigmatic book. *Nature* is not a naturalist's monograph nor a metaphysician's scheme; it is a rehearsal of the expressive and reflexive movements of awakening that the book itself only provides the place and the occasion for.

We must be careful, therefore, not to demand an inappropriate consistency here. *Nature,* in spite of all its romantic rhetoric of symbol and organicism, does not exactly represent itself: it should not be taken at face value. The letters of *Nature* commit themselves to a grand misrepresentation which it is the business of the reader to dissolve. This, it seems to me, is what Harold Bloom has in mind when he styles Emerson's first book as "a blandly dissociative apocalypse, in which everything is a cheerful error, indeed a misreading, starting with the title, which says 'Nature' but means 'Man.' "[4]

There will be occasion further on to revise somewhat Bloom's interesting formulation, but here he provides us with our point of departure. Representing the most Emersonian tradition of Emerson criticism, Bloom looks not to nature for the meaning of *Nature* but to its revisioning. Emerson, we remember, wondered out loud whether nature was not in the long run "only in the apocalypse of the mind" (CW, I, 29). And increasingly some of Emerson's acutest commentators have wondered whether Emerson's anomalous little book is not more of the same. So Packer finds in *Nature* a "prescription for apocalypse," while Maurice Gonnaud remarks that the mood of *Nature* rises to "the sublime and apocalyptic."[5] In his spiritual biography of Emerson, Joel Porte devotes some twenty pages to an exploration of the apocalyptic dimensions of *Nature,* demonstrating the promise of an angle of vision essentially bookish and biblical in character.[6] For *Nature* clearly, unlike its namesake, was not created in the beginning or *ex nihilo.* Rather it begins where many of our greatest books do, in the middle of things, between a looking back and a looking forward, intent on saying something new but constrained to using a language that has said so many times before. Nature does not provide that language, but books can. And for the kind of language Emerson needed, in New England in the early part of the nineteenth century, there was still really only one place to turn—and that was the Christian Bible. Perhaps this is why some of Emerson's first readers were quicker to recognize its essential design than most of us today. Jones Very, the Transcendentalist visionary and gadfly, jotted down references to the Book of Revelation in the margins of his copy and Thomas Carlyle professed to see in it "the true Apocalypse . . . when the 'open secret' becomes revealed to a man."[7] But, as Porte has pointed out, no early reader of *Nature* was more discerning in his judgment than Oliver Wendell Holmes. "It may be remembered," Holmes wrote in 1884, "that Calvin, in his Commentary on the New Testament, stopped when he came to the Book of the Revelation. He found it full of difficulties which he did not care to encounter. Yet, considered only as a poem, the vision of Saint John is full of noble imagery and wonderful beauty. 'Nature' is the Book of Revelation of our St. Radulphus."[8]

The Book of Revelation is not the only biblical model Holmes finds refracted in *Nature,* and his playful tone might lead us to wonder how seriously his claim should be taken. But his witticisms aside, Holmes's literary instincts led him close to the heart of Emerson's *Nature.* It may be that his levity has proved something of a decoy, but whatever the reason, this is an area which critics are still just skirting.

No book made so lasting an impression on Emerson's imagination as the Bible, and no American classic is more completely under its sway than *Nature.* The first part of this statement will probably meet with little resistance: the second may raise some eyebrows. But this is the view to which the following pages must finally lead. To make that view more plausible I will carry out my demonstration at three interrelated levels: the formal or outer properties of *Nature,* the interior or psychological sense of *Nature,* and finally the role of the reader in *Nature.*

I am indebted to Joel Porte's engaging discussion for opening the way and laying much of the intertextual groundwork for the interpretation which follows. His documentation of *Nature*'s more or less explicit biblical allusions and antecedents, as well as his recognition of some of its thematic parallels to the Book of Revelation, places my own treatment of *Nature*'s formal dependence on Scripture on firmer footing. But there is even more of the Bible in *Nature* than a few explicit allusions to Luke and Saint Paul and a few parallels in imagery and theme. *Nature*'s language and imagery drew deeply on the Bible. It is true that much of it is attenuated or "submerged," to use Porte's term. Indeed Emerson goes out of his way to cover up or naturalize many of his biblical dues, but as we shall see, the cover-up itself is most revealing.

What I will argue for here is something more radical, in fact, than a claim for influence, since then my argument would rest on little more than analogy. The relationship of *Nature* to the Bible is more intimate and also more complicated than that. *Nature* grows out of the Bible, recapitulates its structure, and participates in its vision. Like the Bible, *Nature* consists of a series of revelations and revisions culminating in a world- and word-rending apocalypse. Viewed traditionally, revelation is not what the Bible is about merely, or what it leads to—the Bible *is* Revelation from beginning to end. And this design is the one which Emerson found most essential to re-present in *Nature*. Here for the first time, he announces a formula for revelation which becomes the leitmotif of his addresses and essays throughout the next decade. There this formula begins to assume a quasi-secular cast: here in *Nature* it still retains the marks and vestiges of its apocalyptic origins.

Itself a revision, *Nature* thus salvages its key from the fact of previous revision, and having done so it enunciates its own method and enacts its own progress. Like the biblical revelations from which it arises and distinguishes itself, *Nature* is essentially self-referential: it consists in the visions and revisions, the types and anti-types, of its own prospective word. *Nature* then looks to itself, not to nature. The question is not what it means but how it does so. It is self-reflective, its structure one of self-referral. It consists of a series of readings which, moving in a circle, overlap, revise, and in the process, erase themselves in a manner which looks ahead to the essay "Circles." *Nature,* we might say, is the process of reading over itself, but it refuses to commit itself to any particular view or vision. Aspiring to a kind of pure vision that knows none of the limits of previous visions, it rests in the faith that only when such perfect vision dawns will the "new heaven and earth" be realized. In this way, toward that horizon, the site of Emerson's apocalypse moves from nature through the text to the mind of the reader.

1 Prevision

*Each age, it is found, must write its own
books; or rather, each generation for the next
succeeding. The books of an older period
will not fit this.* (CW, I, 56)

*We too must write Bibles, to unite again the
heavens and the earthly world.* (W, IV, 290)

No American writer since Jonathan Edwards is more thoroughly
steeped in the Christian Bible than Ralph Waldo Emerson. Not
only did it shape his earliest values and beliefs, and provide his
first mythology, it conditioned the language he spoke. In this, of
course, he was by no means singular. The New England of Emerson's time was still very much a biblical culture.[1] The Bible was
the book—Blake called it "The Great Code"—that generated the
value and resonance in American words. It had settled down into
the bedrock of the New England mind, and all other texts were
only the sediment that had settled unevenly on top of it. No one
knew this better than Emerson: "The Bible itself," he wrote, "is
like an old Cremona; it has been played upon by the devotion of
thousands of years until every word and particle is public and

tunable" (W, VIII, 173–74).[2] Emerson's writings, early and late, are peppered with allusions to Scripture: some explicit, some oblique, and some purely ironic.[3] But the overall effect is of a prose dancing just within earshot of the idioms and rhythms of the King James Bible. For a writer and orator with Emerson's upbringing and early enthusiasm for the power of words, there was really very little choice: poet and preacher alike looked to the Bible as their common inheritance.

But Emerson, we have to remember, was both poet *and* preacher—though of the first he was only the "husky" variety, and he was the second only for a relatively brief period in his career (L, I, 435). Nevertheless, from the fall of 1826, when he was approbated to preach, till the end of the next decade, when he did so for the last time, Emerson had written and delivered 171 sermons, some as many as ten or twenty times. While many of the sermons follow the not untypical Unitarian practice of being somewhat latitudinarian in their choice of subjects—in addition to his more clearly biblical themes, Emerson preached on such topics as "Astronomy," "Summer," and "Hymn Books"— they generally keep to the traditional practice of beginning with a scriptural text. The journals from his college years up to the time he resigned his pastorate at the Second Church in 1832 contain numerous references to scriptural passages, some in lists that run on for several pages. Emerson knew his Bible well—so well that he was a bit chagrined and amused when a Bible-toting sea captain on his 1833 voyage to Europe stumped him in a short biblical quiz: "The good Captain rejoices much in my ignorance. He confounded me the other day about the book in the Bible where God was not mentioned and last night upon St. Paul's shipwreck" (JMN, IV, 111).

The significance of Scripture was not, of course, as straightforward for Emerson as it appears to have been for his blustery sea captain. For Emerson, as for many of his liberally educated contemporaries, the Bible had become the main battleground between the old and new views. Emerson was only a Harvard junior when Professor Edward Everett returned from abroad loaded down with the results of some of the new "higher criticism" of the Bible.[4] From Everett's course on Greek literature and from the lectures on French literature given by George Ticknor, another recent initiate into the German criticism, Emerson caught wind of the great upheaval in traditional biblical studies then in progress on the Continent.[5] Like many of his classmates, Emerson listened with rapt attention to Everett's lectures and addresses, though he seems to have been more enamored of Everett's oratorical brilliance than of the substance of his views.

In the province of theology, Emerson was still the devoted admirer of the Reverend Dr. William Ellery Channing, popular leader of the Boston Unitarian establishment. Though to many young divinity students Channing represented an ideal freedom from creed, he adhered to a belief in Jesus' unique authority and the historical authenticity of the Gospels, a few miracles excepting. The Bible was still the authentic and exclusive Word of God. "Nature," Channing insisted, "had always been found insufficient to teach men the great doctrines which Revelation inculcated."[6]

But already in his undergraduate years, Emerson was being buffeted by the crosswinds of religious crisis that Stephen Whicher first called attention to.[7] In spite of Channing's influence, Emerson could still write to his aunt, Mary Moody Emerson, that Christian Revelation "has not for me the same exclusive and extraordinary claims it has for many. I hold Reason to be a prior Revelation, and that they do not contradict each other."[8] The incipient crisis over biblical authority would be brought to a head, however, by a more personal connection to the higher criticism. Emerson's older brother William, against the recommendation of Channing, had decided to go to Göttingen to study theology and biblical criticism under Eichhorn and other scholars then popularizing a more scientific study of religion. William's letters to his brother betray the excitement sparked by all the lectures he was hearing on demythologizing. By the time of his voyage home in 1825, William had fully relinquished his earlier views on the Bible and with them his vocation to the ministry. The gauntlet had passed to Waldo—that, at least, is the way his Aunt Mary seems to have seen it—and it was now his responsibility to uphold the family's ministerial tradition. In any case, William's apostasy seems to have galvanized in his younger brother a desire to champion the old faith. In an 1826 letter to his aunt, Waldo wrote:

> You have received the boding letter I writ from Cambridge
> concerning German faith. I am anxious to have sight enow
> to study theology in this regard. The objections the German
> scholars have proposed attack the foundations of external
> evidence, and so give up the internal to historical specula-
> tors and pleasant doubters. . . . But it were vile and supine
> to sit and be astonished without exploring the strength of
> the enemy. If heaven gives me sight, I will dedicate it to
> this cause. (J, II, 83–85)

Though Emerson's resolve is undoubtedly firm, his inherited
creed had placed him and many other young Unitarians in what
seemed an untenable intellectual position. Legatees of Scottish
common-sense philosophy as well as the empiricism of David
Hume, they were at the same time called upon to uphold the Unitarian belief in miracles. For many intellectuals, the only way out of
this dilemma was the wholesale rejection of miracles and, with
them, the historicity and exclusive claims of the Bible. Emerson,
however, took a rather more novel route: instead of shrinking
down the province of the miraculous, he expanded it to cover the
whole continuum of time and space. More and more over the next
ten years, and particularly after he resigned his ministry, Emerson evinced a tendency to abandon the whole debate about particular miracles in favor of a vision of the ongoing miracle of existence.
As regards the Bible, this audacious move had the desirable consequence of saving the validity of Revelation, in spite of the fact that
it also entailed a rejection of its exclusive authority. "Bible" suddenly switched from singular to plural, though retaining an upper-
case usage, and with the Western world's growing awareness of the
scriptures of other cultures, Emerson and many of his generation
could speak with increasing ease of the Bibles of the world.[9]
Granting the sacredness of other peoples' scriptures, however,
was only one consequence, a natural one, of Emerson's rejection of
the exclusivist claims of the Christian revelation. His heady de-
mocratization of the sacred had far more radical implications for
his career. No longer was revelation confined to the remote past
or to the reports of other people. As the barriers of time and place

were thrown down, nature itself could be received as the perpetual, up-to-the-minute announcement of the divine.

Emerson's fascination with the mystique of nature had deep roots in his childhood and in his own contemplative nature. But if any one person deserves credit for instilling in the young Waldo a reverence for the Creation, it was his indefatigable Aunt Mary. At twenty Emerson wrote to a friend from the White Mountains:

> I am seeking to put myself on a footing of old acquaintance with Nature, as a poet should,—but the fair divinity is somewhat shy of my advances, and I confess I cannot find myself quite as perfectly at home on the rock and in the wood, as my ancient, and I may say, infant aspirations led me to expect. My aunt, (of whom I think you have heard before and who is alone among women,) has spent a great part of her life in the country, is an idolator of Nature, and counts but a small number who merit the privilege of dwelling among the mountains. The coarse thrifty cit profanes the grove by his presence—and she was anxious that her nephew might hold high and reverential notions regarding it (as) the temple where God and the Mind are to be studied and adored and where the fiery soul can begin a premature communication with other worlds. (L, I, 133)

This kind of nature mysticism, though pitched at an extraordinarily high level in Mary Moody Emerson, was by no means unique in New England Calvinism, as some of the treatises of Jonathan Edwards suggest.[10] Indeed, it is not unlikely that Mary's own avid reading of Edwards was in part responsible for her contemplative orientation to nature—her inclination, that is, to peruse nature for glimpses of the other world. And it is in this respect, at least, that she and Waldo may be seen as Edwards's direct heirs.[11] Though Emerson does not in these early years exhibit toward nature the kind of passionate yearning his aunt does, by the time of his visit to the Jardin des Plantes at Paris on his first European tour, in 1833, he has plainly begun to feel its undeniable stirrings:

> The Universe is a more amazing puzzle than ever as you glance along this bewildering series of animated forms,— .... Not a form so grotesque, so savage, nor so beautiful but is an expression of some property inherent in man the observer,—an occult relation between the very scorpions and man. I feel the centipede in me—cayman, carp, eagle, and fox. I am moved by strange sympathies, I say continually "I will be a naturalist." (JMN, IV, 199–200)

What is revealing about this famous entry, and significant for the light it sheds on *Nature,* is the character of Emerson's inspiration to study nature in more detail. It is not so much the particular organisms themselves that arouse his interest as their inexplicable *reference* to him. Already his attention has shifted from the facts of his observation to the mysterious language by which they are conveyed. Nature has ceased for him to be the arena of brute process, if such it ever was, and has transformed itself into a language that must be deciphered.

The Book of Nature

To conceive nature as a set of signifiers seems to have been as natural for Waldo as it was for his favorite aunt. In New England it finds its clearest precedent, as we have seen, in some of Edwards's lesser-known writings. And it was but one short step from seeing nature as significant to reading nature as a book—a conception which had, of course, a wide circulation among the various writers whom Emerson collected under the rubric "modern philosophy." The book metaphor itself, however, seems to derive from homiletic rhetoric and the mystico-philosophical speculation of the Latin Middle Ages.[12] By the flowering of the Renaissance the phrase had slipped into common usage, so that Sir Thomas Browne is on familiar ground when he writes: "Thus there are *two Books* from whence I collect my Divinity; besides that written one of God, another of His servant Nature, that universal and publick

Manuscript, that lies expans'd unto the Eyes of all: those that
never saw him in the one, have discover'd Him in the other."[13] Of
the Renaissance and late Renaissance writers who made the deepest lasting impression on Emerson—Montaigne, Bacon, Herbert,
and Milton—all found the metaphor of the book to be a ready
handle for articulating their views on nature.[14] In 1833 Emerson
made an entry into his journal which clearly looks forward to
Nature: "Bacon said man is the minister and interpreter of nature: he is so in more respects than one. He is not only to explain
the sense of each passage but the scope and argument of the whole
book" (JMN, IV, 95). But of the many sources in the early nineteenth century which might have suggested this conception to the
young Emerson, none generated as much excitement as Sampson
Reed, the Swedenborgian druggist whose graduate oration Emerson heard at Harvard in the summer of 1821 (JMN, I, 293–94). In
1826 Emerson extolled Reed's recently published treatise *Observations on the Growth of the Mind,* which, he said, "has to my mind
the aspect of a revelation" (JMN, III, 44–45). One of the elements
of Reed's thought for which Emerson seems to have felt special
sympathy is its apocalyptic streak—its inclination, as Porte
points out, to see nature as a direct revelation from God.[15] But
Reed's little book was also Emerson's fullest early exposure to the
Swedenborgian idea of correspondences, which was to have such
an important impact on the "Language" section of *Nature.*[16]

The Swedenborgian whose formulations would surface most
clearly in *Nature* , however, was not Reed but an obscure French
author named Guillaume Oegger. In July of 1835, Emerson transcribed several pages of Oegger's work *The True Messiah; or the
Old and New Testament Examined According to the Principles of
the Language of Nature,* among which was this sentence appearing in only slightly altered form in *Nature:* "The visible creation
then cannot must not . . . be anything but the exterior circumference of the invisible and metaphysical world, and material objects are necessarily kinds of scoriae of the substantial thoughts
of the Creator; scoriae which must always preserve an exact
relation to their first origin; in other words visible nature must
have a spiritual and moral side" (JMN, V, 66).[17] There is one
last debt to mention in this short catalogue, which, while it

might not have suggested to Emerson his developing views on the textuality of nature, certainly must have reinforced, perhaps even catalyzed, them. This was Carlyle. After his visit to Craigenputtock at the end of his European trip in 1833, Emerson had been eager to read the forthcoming installments of *Sartor Resartus* then appearing in *Fraser's Magazine*. In one of the many wild climaxes of Teufelsdröckh's visionary ravings, the chapter famously entitled "Natural Supernaturalism," Emerson would have read: "We speak of the Volume of Nature: and truly a Volume it is,—whose Author and Writer is God."[18]

Channing, we remember, like most traditional Christians— and this includes Coleridge and the Swedenborgians—was unwilling to allow that the book of nature was adequate to inculcate the truths of the moral life. By 1833, if not long before, Emerson, it seems, was toying with the thought that it might be. "Nature is a language and every new fact that we learn is a new word; but rightly seen, taken all together it is not merely a language < but a scripture which contains the whole truth.> but the language put together into a most significant and universal book. I wish to learn the language not that I may know a new set of nouns and verbs but that I may read the great book which is written in that tongue" (JMN, IV, 95). Emerson discreetly canceled from his journal the logical conclusion of his faith in the fidelity of nature, but as we can see, it is plainly legible in his thoughts. While his faith in the readability of that grand text—the extent to which its words could be viewed as "constant analogies" participating in a "radical correspondence" with spiritual things—would become more equivocal as he grew increasingly disenchanted with the fixed Swedenborgian scheme, he never seems to have abandoned his basic faith in the spiritual significance of nature. In 1836 he is quite confident that "every natural fact is a symbol of some spiritual fact" and that nature, as a whole, "is the symbol of spirit" (CW, I, 17–18).

What is interesting to point out about the traditional view of nature as a text, whether in Emerson's writings or those of his predecessors, is that in it nature is entirely subordinated to Scripture.[19] It is not objectively conceived, perhaps it never is; it is preconceived—according to the model provided by Scripture. Nature, in this view, has no independent reality apart from its status as a book. It is assumed that nature's processes and phenomena mean something to man and that they may be more or less deciphered by applying to them certain rules of reading and interpretation. Nature itself does not, of course, supply these rules. Nature does not present to us examples of "the symbol" or "sign" or "allegory" or "metaphor"—all figures that Emerson employs without hesitation for nature as a whole or one of its many parts. If we ask where this richly figured nature comes from, we are led not to nature, but away from it—to the conventions of language and, specifically, to Scripture. Nature, we begin to recognize, is really just a mask for Scripture, and nowhere is this easier to see than in the "Language" section of *Nature,* where etymologies ("*Spirit* primarily means *wind*") and emblems ("a snake is subtle spite") frequently have a biblical origin or sanction, where "the seed of a plant" calls up the words of Saint Paul in 1 Corinthians 15.44, where "the laws of moral nature answer to those of matter as face to face in a glass" (1 Cor. 13.12). Indeed, here and elsewhere, there sound in *Nature* the distinct echoes of Scripture.

While Emerson frequently appears to be the willing believer of his own misrepresentations, he is hardly unaware of his debts. In a sermon called "Summer," which he first delivered in 1829, and which adumbrates the themes of *Nature* in several important ways, he clearly acknowledges that debt:

But there is more in nature than beauty; there is more to be seen than the outward eye perceives; there is more to be heard than the pleasant rustle of corn. There is the language of its everlasting analogies, by which it seems to be the prophet and the monitor of the race of man. The Scripture is always appealing to the tree and the flower and the grass as the emblems of our mortal estate. It was the history of man in the beginning, and it is the history of man now. Man is like the flower of the field. In the morning he is like grass that groweth up; in the evening he is cut down and withereth. There is nothing in external nature but is an emblem, a hieroglyphic of something in us. (YES, 44)

Though Emerson does not even concede the primacy of Scripture over the Book of Nature here, he does go so far as to suggest that we have scriptural sanction for seeing nature as a book of emblems. But we need not take only Emerson's word for it—the Bible provides its own license in Romans 1.19 and following, where Saint Paul argues that even pagans cannot be excused from some knowledge of God: "Because that which may be known of God is manifest in them; for God hath shown it unto them. For the invisible things of him from the creation of the world are clearly seen, being understood by the things that are made, even his eternal power and Godhead."

One of the most interesting clues for how nature ought best to be read is contained in Emerson's use of the word *type*. Occasionally the word crops up in the journals and essays with its common meaning of *kind* or sometimes as representative symbol, but in *Nature,* where it appears several times, Emerson leans on it in a revealing way. The blue sky "in which the private earth is buried, the sky with its eternal calm, and full of everlasting orbs, is the type of Reason." And: "This immediate dependence of language upon nature, this conversion of an outward phenomenon into a type of somewhat in human life, never loses its power to affect us" (CW, I, 18–20). Here the context suggests that he is also drawing on the technical sense the term has in biblical criticism—a sense which Emerson would have had trouble ignoring given his theological and biblical training. In the long tradition of biblical exegesis and interpretation, *type* refers to some symbol, event, or other configuration in the Hebrew Bible which is viewed by later interpreters as predicting or foreshadowing a similar configuration in the New Testament. Not only has typological interpretation influenced the viewpoints of many later interpreters; it is characteristic of the way the New Testament views itself, as its many backward references to the Hebrew Bible, particularly in such books as the Letter to the Hebrews and Revelation, suggest.

For Northrop Frye the correspondence between type and antitype is so basic to the structure of the Christian Bible that Old Testament and New Testament "form a double mirror, each reflecting the other but neither the world outside."[20] What connects these widely separated biblical accounts is, of course, history itself or, more accurately, the sacred history of God's plan. In *Nature*, however, history has been effectively annulled—the relationship between type and anti-type is no longer temporal, but spatial or perhaps we might want to say psychological. The outer world constitutes a book of types which look within, not ahead, for their revelation. In and of itself, this transposition of typology from a historical to a natural context is not all that unorthodox. In his miscellaneous notebook, *Images or Shadows of Divine Things,* Edwards defended types from the natural world as a simple extension of biblical typology.[21] Emerson's inclination, evinced in his sermon "Summer," to find types in nature that function analogously to the types in the Bible thus has a quite exact precedent in Edwards. Emerson casts off from the orthodox shore, however, when he offers to supplant the revelation of sacred history with the ongoing revelations of nature: "Why should not we also enjoy an original relation to the universe? Why should not we have a poetry and philosophy of insight and not of tradition, and a religion by revelation to us, and not the history of theirs?" (CW, I, 7).

Despite this ostensible rejection of the primacy of the historical Revelation, it is interesting that *Nature* does not abandon the one mode of interpretation peculiar to it. For the most part, the reigning figure of speech in *Nature,* as it is in many romantic texts, is the symbol, and not the old biblical one of type; yet Emerson retains the biblical usage. What this suggests is that, while he is anxious to dissolve the distance between type and anti-type, he is not willing to diminish the weight of the connection. The staging of nature differs from that of the Bible, but the purport is basically the same. Symbol or type, in the end both yield to Revelation. Nowhere is this better seen than in the unsettling and prophetic declaration Emerson made to his aunt in 1826: "It is one of the *feelings* of modern philosophy, that it is wrong to regard ourselves so much in a *historical* light as we do, putting Time between God us; and that it were fitter to account every moment of the existence of the Universe as a new Creation, and *all* as a revelation proceeding each moment from the Divinity to the mind of the observer" (L, I, 174).

To develop the character of the eternal revelation envisaged here is the purpose of the next chapter, but for now it is enough to establish that whenever (whether at the end of historical time or in each passing moment), or wherever (whether in the skies above or in the mind of the observer), revelation occurs the medium through which it makes itself known is best represented as a book. Nature is undoubtedly the older book to Emerson, and superior, but he owes his idea of it and his expression of it to a model he could only get from culture. So nature is a "grand cipher," a "text," the "present expositor of the divine mind." It is even compared in its "ministry" to "the figure of Jesus," God's Word: "it is a remoter and inferior incarnation of God, a projection of God in the unconscious" (CW, I, 38). Like the Bible's Book of Revelation, nature is a book of pictures, a kind of divine emblem book. And like that book, this one is not easy to decipher. "Have mountains, and waves, and skies, no significance but what we conciously give them, when we employ them as emblems of our thoughts? The world is emblematic" (CW, I, 21).

Besides the literal sense, nature's words convey a spiritual sense, so that " 'every object rightly seen, unlocks a new faculty of the soul' " (CW, I, 23). Emerson borrows from Coleridge for this last formulation, but behind this idea stands a whole tradition of biblical interpretation represented by such diverse commentators as Swedenborg, Thomas Aquinas, and Augustine. Distinctions aside, the assumption that scriptural texts convey several levels of meaning simultaneously naturally places a special burden of responsibility upon the interpreter. Like the Book of Revelation, the Book of Nature does not deliver up its secret sense to unwary readers. So the same "fundamental law of criticism" must apply: " 'Every scripture is to be interpreted by the same spirit which gave it forth' " Only "a life in harmony with nature . . . will purge the eyes to understand her text," and the result will be that "we may come to know the primitive sense of the permanent objects of nature, so that the world shall be to us an open book, and every form significant of its hidden life and final cause" (CW, I, 23). The phrase "open book" has been drifting so long in common parlance that most of us may no longer know where it comes from, but Emerson probably did. Underlying his oblique allusion is the text from Revelation 20.12: "And I saw the dead small and great, stand before God, and the books were opened; and another book was opened, which is the book of life. And the dead were judged out of those things which were written in the books, according to their works."

Clues such as these leave us in little doubt as to how we should look at nature and what might be gained from a proper perusal. The equation of nature with World and with the Body of Spirit bears the faint traces of its earlier formulation as Christ with Word and with God's Incarnation. But what then is the status of the book called *Nature* which Emerson, the man, composed? In his introduction to volume 1 of Emerson's *Collected Works,* Robert Spiller refers to it as a "new testament." While such a designation may have been intended mainly for its suggestive value, there is a sense in which it is strictly accurate, if we conceive nature, as Oegger seems to have done, as the "true Messiah." *Nature* then is the testimony or testament of this new revelation. If this claim sounds too extreme, we should recall that for Emerson, as for many of the Romantics, the biblical books were the work of inspired poets, indeed that "the religions of the world are the ejaculations of a few imaginative men" (CW, III, 20). Commentators such as Spiller, therefore, are not far off when they place what is otherwise a rather anomalous book squarely in the category of religious literature.[22]

Several critics have shed light on some of the religious affiliations of *Nature* through investigations of its debt to the sermon structure. F. O. Matthiessen remarked long ago that, though Emerson had abandoned the pulpit, *Nature* and "The American Scholar" still make use of the formal logical divisions of his early sermons.[23] And Warner Berthoff has discussed the obligation of Emerson's rhetorical architecture in *Nature* to sermon structure in general.[24] In his book *Literary Transcendentalism,* Lawrence Buell provides an informative discussion of the continuities between Unitarian rhetoric—especially its two favorite forms of discourse, conversation and pulpit preaching—and the literary performances of the Transcendentalists, and then goes on to make the crucial observation that the shift from Unitarian to Transcendentalist expression was "a movement from sermon to scripture." For Buell this shift from sermon as model for literary making to scripture resulted from the rejection of the ministry and the

exclusivist claims of the Christian Bible. But like the rhetoric of
the Unitarian sermon, Transcendentalist prose continued to echo
the rhythms and styles of the Bible. In particular, Buell notes its
reliance on figurative expression, multiplicity of demonstration,
what he calls "rhapsodic flow and vagueness," and an "interfusion
of poetic feeling and moral tone."[25] Among these, the feature of
ancient scriptures which he singles out for extended comment is
reiteration—the prevalence in American romantic texts of "catalogue rhetoric" similar to that found, for example, in the Psalms
or other Wisdom books of the Bible. Emerson, like his contemporaries, is fond of this device and uses it to good effect in *Nature:*

> The moral influence of nature upon every individual is that
> amount of truth which it illustrates to him.
>
> Who can estimate this?
>
> Who can guess how much firmness the sea-beaten rock has
> taught the fisherman?
>
> How much tranquility has been reflected to man from the
> azure sky, over whose unspotted deeps the winds forever-
> more drive flocks of stormy clouds, and leave no wrinkle or
> stain?
>
> How much industry and providence and affection we have
> caught from the pantomime of brutes?
>
> What a searching preacher of self-command is the varying
> phenomenon of Health! (CW, I, 26–27)

The stanzaic representation here is of course my own, but it
serves to define and articulate the paratactical structure that
underlies this passage. It consists simply of a loosely arranged
series of rhetorical questions in parallel construction. What connects these linguistic units is not semantic: shuffle the questions
and the meaning does not suffer. The connections are more elusive and have more to do with rhythm and sound, it seems, than
sense. Such a style is clearly not suitable for logical disquisition;
it is, however, well adapted to prophetic oracle, aphorism, or proc-

lamation, as in the Bible, where the authority of the utterance lies inside, not outside, its structure.

The kind of attention to stylistic issues evinced by a critic like Buell leads inexorably back to the Bible. What is a little surprising is that after a nod in this direction Buell all but abandons this interesting lead with the remark that "the concept of scripture alone was not a sufficient guide" after all. Contending that Emerson found scripture too "fragmentary" and deploring Alcott's "Orphic Sayings," the Transcendentalist's "nearest attempt" at scripture-making, as "a disaster," Buell goes on to a more lengthy (and more conventional) consideration of nature "as a model for literary form."[26]

As Buell himself acknowledges in the next chapter, upon closer examination there are, however, few "models" in nature a poet can apply his pen to, but one that the criticism of romanticism bases much of its theorizing on is the idea of the microcosmic form. It is true that of all Emerson's writings his essay "The Poet" epitomizes this idea, but it is first articulated in *Nature:* "Every particular in nature, a leaf, a drop, a crystal, a moment of time is related to the whole, and partakes of the perfection of the whole. Each particle is a microcosm, and faithfully renders the likeness of the world" (CW, I, 27). Art then establishes its own claim to fidelity by being itself a microcosm, by expressing within its own structure the same harmony, the same relation of parts to whole, that unites the parts of nature. "A work of art is an abstract or epitome of the world. It is the result or expression of nature, in miniature" (CW, I, 16–17). The claim for the "organic" basis of the microcosmic form rests partly on the integrity of its structure, its wholeness; but where does the imputed isomorphism between different microcosmic forms come from? It rests, suggests Emerson, on the "analogous impression" they make on the mind—on analogy! In fact, nature does not present analogies—man sees them. Actually the same might be said of nature's ostensible wholeness—is it there or is it a function of reading? Once again we are faced with an interesting misrepresentation. Behind the natural microcosm is something very like Coleridge's symbol—a figure of speech which "partakes of the Reality which it renders intelligible"—and behind Emerson's (and Coleridge's) symbol, as

I have suggested above, is something very like the old biblical type.[27] That Emerson was all along thinking "Bible" when he was writing "Nature" is further suggested by his later comment that natural objects "are really parts of a symmetrical universe, like words of a sentence; and if their true order is found, the poet can read their divine significance orderly as in a Bible" (W, VIII, 14).

No one can deny that Emerson built *Nature* after the model of nature, at least ostensibly. But what exactly does that mean? Which nature and where? It is worth asking—if in fact nature provides the model for *Nature*—what the model is for Emerson's conception of nature? As I have tried to suggest above, Emerson's nature is a proxy; everywhere within and behind it may be described the pages and outlines of a book, and not any book—but a book whose symbols, properly used, open out into revelation. *Nature* then constitutes a true isomorph of nature in the sense that they both reflect the design and concerns of Revelation. These reasons alone are sufficient to persuade us that readers such as Carlyle and Holmes were on to something important when they styled *Nature* a latter-day Book of Revelation.

The Book of Revelation

To call *Nature* a Book of Revelation is to place it within a genre of biblical writing known technically as "apocalypse," which, in addition to its most famous instance in the New Testament Book of Revelation, includes the Book of Daniel, parts of the books of Isaiah and Zechariah, and many apocryphal texts, both Jewish and Christian, as well. The English title of Saint John's book of visions derives from the Latin *revelatio*, which is itself a translation of the Greek word *apokalupsis*. "Apocalypse" or "Revelation" is literally an "unveiling" or a disclosure of that which was previously concealed or unknown. While the genre as a whole resists tight definition, one of its distinctive features is the pervasive use of figurative language—arcane symbols used to represent the events leading up to the last days and the ushering in of God's Kingdom. The editors of the Oxford Bible, for example, refer to the Revelation of Saint John, with its mystic trumpets and seals, its horsemen, and its choruses of angels, as "an inspired picture book." In this respect, no book of the Christian Bible is so continuously preoccupied with the issues of meaning and representation as Saint John's Apocalypse, and this is part of the reason why no book of the Bible has had such a seminal influence on the literary, as well as the religious, imagination of the West.[28]

Although the word *apocalypse* has come increasingly to refer in contemporary usage to any sudden cataclysm or wholesale destruction, this is not its biblical significance. There, as M. H. Abrams rightly insists, it refers to the passing of the old order *and* the creation of the new.[29] The key text, itself a revision of Isaiah 65.17–25, occurs at Revelation 21.1–5: "And I saw a new heaven and a new earth; for the first heaven and the first earth were passed away, . . . And he that sat upon the throne said, Behold, I make all things new. And he said unto me, Write, for these words are true and faithful." The crucial event of apocalypse is the double one of destruction and creation. The spectacular progress of annihilation for which Saint John's visions are so justly memorable—"and the sun became black . . . and the moon became like blood; and the stars of heaven fell unto the earth . . . and the heaven departed as a scroll"—only paves the way for the final revelation of Jesus Christ and the creation of the new heaven and earth (Rev. 6.12–14).

Unlike the Bible as a whole, which begins with the creation of the world and ends with its consummation, the Book of Revelation begins with the consummation and ends with a creation. This suggests that, though biblical time is generally conceived as linear, there is a sense in which it curves back on itself. With the Second Coming of Christ from on high, the world is redeemed and transformed into a paradise reminiscent of Eden, replete with flowing water and its own tree of life (Rev. 22.1–5).[30] Temporally, the visions of Saint John move from past (Rev. 1.1–20) through present (2.1–3.22) to future. The bulk of his visions, however (Rev. 4.1–22.5), look forward to the events of the millennium and the last days. They consist of a series of revelations to him of the events to come and their relation to the Last Judgment and the final revelation of Christ.

There is no point in pressing the structural comparison too far, but it is easy enough to see that *Nature* roughly conforms to a similar pattern. Unlike the "Divinity School Address" which was to generate such a furor two years later, and which begins with a passage deeply imbued with the airs of paradise, *Nature* does not begin at the beginning, in Man's prelapsarian state, but somewhere in the middle of biblical time, after the Fall but before the Apocalypse. Emerson first sees the way John does, retrospectively; his vision then quickly shifts to present time, where it flares to its fullest in the famous epiphany in the "Nature" section; but from the section entitled "Commodity," where Emerson takes up his inquiry once again and looks forward to "the final cause of the world," until "Prospects," the movement of *Nature* is all prospective. This entire progression from "Nature" to "Prospects" also consists of a series of minor epiphanies or revelations that look forward to the consummation of nature in "Spirit" and the possibility of new vision in "Prospects." As in the Book of Revelation, the crux of *Nature* is the sequence of dissolution, when the world's "outlines and surfaces become transparent," and advent, when God will "go forth anew into the creation." And just as Saint John's Revelation culminates in the creation of a new heaven and earth, Emerson's culminates in his famous exhortation: "Build, therefore, your own world." The rhapsodic finale of *Nature,* concluding with the allusion to Luke 17, is itself a miniature apocalypse—"the sordor and filths of nature" giving way to "the advancing spirit." While this passage is displaced from its original context, naturalized thoroughly, and pruned of its biblical allusions, it is difficult not to perceive its messianic aura.

> As when the summer comes from the south, the snowbanks melt, and the face of the earth becomes green before it, so shall the advancing spirit create its ornaments along its path, and carry with it the beauty it visits, and the song which enchants it; it shall draw beautiful faces, and warm hearts, and wise discourse, and heroic acts, around its way, until evil is no more seen. (CW, I, 45)

The Divine Marriage

In his influential study *Natural Supernaturalism,* Abrams singles out two "key images" in the Book of Revelation. One is the image of the "new heaven and new earth" we have been discussing; the other is the apocalyptic marriage first announced in Revelation 19.7 ("for the marriage of the Lamb is come, and his wife hath made herself ready") and developed in Revelation 21 ("And I, John, saw the holy city, new Jerusalem, coming down from God out of heaven, prepared as a bride adorned for her husband"), which coincides with the new creation and signals the formation of an eternal covenant between God and his people. While the marriage motif is highlighted here in Revelation, it is one of the Bible's most pervasive and fundamental tropes, governing not only the relationship between God and Israel but also that between Christ and his worshippers.[31] Christian mystics of the Middle Ages and afterwards conceived the relationship between the soul and Christ along the lines of the erotic union between bride and bridegroom as it was represented in the Song of Solomon. To the Western religious imagination, it is an image which has always proved most attractive. For the English and German Romantics, as Abrams has shown, the image was displaced but by no means disowned. There, with the transposition of God from the heavens to the heart, the union between bride and bridegroom was conceived as taking place between nature and the mind of Man. So in Hölderlin's *Hyperion* the inspired poet-hero exhorts Nature this way: "Let all be changed from its Foundations! Let the new world spring from the root of humanity! . . . They will come, Nature, thy men. A rejuvenated people will make thee young again, too, and thou wilt be as its bride. . . . There will be only one beauty; and man and Nature will unite in one all-embracing divinity." And Novalis summed it up for much German philosophy with his declaration that "the higher philosophy is concerned with the marriage of Nature and Mind." In the poetry of the English Romantics the motif of the divine marriage found similar application. In "Dejection: An Ode" Coleridge wrote that "Joy"

is the spirit and the power,
Which, wedding Nature to us, gives in dower
A new Earth and new Heaven,
Undreamt of by the sensual and the proud.

But of the English poets, the one who gave the marriage motif its
most influential formulation was probably Wordsworth. For his
"Prospectus" to "The Recluse," Wordsworth drafted the lines upon
which Abrams builds his argument. Among them is this commonly quoted quatrain:

For the discerning intellect of Man,
When wedded to his goodly universe
In love and holy passion, shall find these
A simple produce of the common day.[32]

In spite of Emerson's early disaffection from Wordsworth, much of
the old poet's influence may still be detected in *Nature,* as Holmes
long ago pointed out.[33] In fact, Porte notes that these very lines
were cited by Emerson in a lecture he gave entitled "The Eye and
Ear" a year after the publication of *Nature.*[34]

The displaced image of a marriage between mind and nature
had so diffused itself into Emerson's native climate of ideas that it
is hard to say exactly where or when he got it. It was part of the
air he breathed. In any case, by 1836 it had become almost a habit
of mind. In July he conceived man as "the point wherein matter
and spirit meet and marry" (JMN, V, 187). In November he remarked that "the world is full of happy marriages of faculty to
object, of means to end; and all of Man marries all of Nature, and
makes it fruitful" (JMN, V, 236). "The universe," he wrote later
in his essay "Experience," "is the bride of the soul" (CW, III, 44).[35]
If the biblical foundations are not still visible in the phrasings of
these citations, they are somewhat more apparent in the most
important use of this motif in *Nature.*

The reason why the world lacks unity, and lies broken and
in heaps, is, because man is disunited with himself. He
cannot be a naturalist, until he satisfies all the demands of

the spirit. Love is as much its demand, as perception. Indeed, neither can be perfect without the other. In the uttermost meaning of the words, thought is devout, and devotion is thought. Deep calls unto deep. But in actual life, the
marriage is not celebrated. (CW, I, 43)

Emerson's direct use of the famous phrase from Psalms 42.7
serves to associate the barrenness of separation between Nature
and Spirit, and between love and perception, with the longing of
the Psalmist for his God. And the passage as a whole ends with
the allusion cited above to the time when God will come again
into his creation. Appearing as it does in the middle of these
messianic passages in *Nature,* this oblique reference to the divine
marriage further brightens the apocalyptic underpinnings of the
final section. But in *Nature* as a whole it is by no means the only
such reference. Though displaced as it is for the other Romantics,
and somewhat attenuated, it underlies and informs the overall
structure of Emerson's book.

We may note that on August 8, 1836, approximately one month
before the appearance of *Nature* in the Boston bookstalls, Emerson wrote to his brother William making reference, among other
things, to "one crack . . . not easy to be soldered or welded" that
still remained in the book he had been preparing (L, II, 32). The
fact that six weeks previously he had informed William of his
plan to write a sequel to *Nature,* which he would call "Spirit," has
suggested to many critics that this must be the location of the
famous "crack"—the great divide between Nature and Spirit (L,
II, 26). As I have suggested above, critics who allege that this was
one gap Emerson never succeeded in mending are undoubtedly on
firm philosophical ground. But there are other methods of repair
than the purely philosophic, in fact many, and these are the ones,
I would contend, that he relied on exclusively. Whether he ever
succeeded is a question worth putting off till the end, but so far we
have seen two such methods—the typological and the symbolic.
The allegory of the divine marriage we may take as the third.

For throughout *Nature,* in fact throughout much of his writing,
Emerson reinvokes the image of the divine marriage as a way of
imaginatively overcoming the separation between Nature and

Spirit. As we have seen, the image is of biblical origin, but in *Nature* Emerson develops it into a kind of allegory or running parable for the life of Man.[36] In ignorance Man looks up to Nature as a child to his mother; but as he grows in self-consciousness his attitude changes, and increasingly he finds in Nature his spouse and mate, until, recognizing in her nothing but his own imperial nature, he places her at his feet and lords it over her. In his later essay entitled "Nature," Emerson recasts this parable in terms of a kind of developmental geometry: "Man is fallen; nature is erect, and serves as a differential thermometer, detecting the presence or absence of the divine sentiment in man. By fault of our dulness and selfishness, we are looking up to nature, but when we are convalescent, nature will look up to us" (CW, III, 104). In his first book, however, the parable retains vestiges of its biblical origins and the three stages of infant, lover, and lord outlined above.

We begin, of course, "embosomed for a season in nature," but it is only the first of man's seasons when he sucks, like a child, at the breast of Nature. Here already the fate of man is prefigured, for Nature's "floods of life . . . invite us by the powers they supply, to action proportioned to nature." The sensuousness of the imagery in this sentence—"embosomed," "floods of life stream around and through us"—introduces the sexual tone that often accompanies Emerson's use of the allegory. But a closer look will reveal that the fertility imagery he draws on so freely here has a biblical feel. "Floods of life," while only an echo of biblical usage (compare Isaiah 44.3), calls up the imagery used throughout the Bible, from Genesis to the Psalms and Prophets to the New Testament, in connection with the Kingdom of God. The image that best epitomizes the paradisal state is the fountain which Emerson invokes in a similar context in "Spirit" (CW, I, 38). "Dry bones" is an obvious borrowing from the famous vision of Ezekiel in Ezekiel 37.1–6. And "wool and flax," while a pervasive idiom in the Bible, may be traced to Proverbs 31.13, where it is used in connection with a portrait of the virtuous woman: "She seeketh wool, and flax, and worketh willingly with her hands." The last image participates in a cluster of associations throughout the Bible that seems to have some bearing on Emerson's use of it here. In both Proverbs and Hosea, where it is used twice (2.5 and 2.9), "wool

and flax" is associated with marriage; though in the case of Hosea, it is connected with Israel depicted as an adulterous wife. In
all cases, however, it stands for clothing—clothing which signifies
the fullness of God's grace and betokens his constancy. It is not
surprising then that Emerson would find it a suitable image here
to remind his readers of God's and Nature's continuing covenant.
But more may be invested in "wool and flax" than just that, since
Emerson, like Carlyle, was very much preoccupied with the whole
question of clothing. Professor Teufelsdröckh entitled his mag-
num opus, we might recall, *Die Kleider, ihr Werden und Wirken*
(*Clothes: Their Origin and Influences*). And this is because he
considered all language and nature itself to be a form of clothing.
To this extent, at least, Emerson himself may be seen as an advocate of and commentator on the "Clothes Philosophy." "The moment our discourse rises above the ground line of familiar facts,
and is inflamed with passion or exalted by thought, it clothes
itself in images." Inspired thought spontaneously "clothes" itself
in its "natural garment," which is why "good writing and brilliant
discourse are perpetual allegories" (CW, I, 20). The virtue of such
expression, whether in the form of type, symbol, or allegory, is
that it means what it says. Properly read, its meaning is transparent, like the stars in the night sky which the writer of *Nature* so
reveres.

The second stage in Emerson's parable begins when Man's natural Mother appears to him as his spouse. This transfiguration,
based always in perception, begins to be suggested, for example,
in the section on "Beauty": "Nature stretcheth out her arms to
embrace man, only let his thoughts be of equal greatness. Willingly does she follow his steps with the rose and the violet, and
bend her lines of grandeur and grace to the decoration of her
darling child. Only let his thoughts be of equal scope, and the
frame will suit the picture" (CW, I, 16). In "Language" Emerson
leans more directly on the marriage motif: "All the facts in natural history taken by themselves, have no value, but are barren
like a single sex. But marry it to human history, and it is full of
life" (CW, I, 19).

By the time the image is invoked in "Discipline," however, the
original relationship has begun to reverse itself: "Nature is thor-

oughly mediate. It is made to serve. It receives the dominion of man as meekly as the ass on which the Savior rode" (CW, I, 25). Man enters the third stage of his progress when Nature becomes for him a mere stepping-stone. Its total subjugation awaits the apocalyptic vision of the Orphic poet at the end, when in the eye of "pure spirit" it becomes "fluid," "volatile," and "obedient." The disappearance of Nature we might cite as the fourth and last stage of Man's progress, but in actuality the parable describes a continuum or, better, a series of expanding circles that encompass and finally entail the world. "More and more, with every thought, does his kingdom stretch over things, until the world becomes, at last, only a realized will,—the double of the man" (CW, I, 25).

Something more may be learned about Nature and the secrets of her apocalypse by the dresses she wears here. It is a matter of some curiosity that of all the seasons Emerson might have picked to show off her "Beauty" he chooses winter, unlike the "Address" he gave two years later and the sermon he gave seven years before, which both luxuriate in summer. We should remember that it was a "January sunset" whose sublimity he treats us to, and it was in "snow puddles" that the revelation came. If we want to write this off as a mere accident of the Journals, perhaps Emerson's own comment about this apparent favoritism of season might give us pause. "The inhabitants of cities suppose that the country landscape is pleasant only half the year. I please myself with observing the graces of the winter scenery, and believe that we are as much touched by it as by the genial influences of summer" (CW, I, 14).

It is true, of course, that winter is not the only phase of nature we witness here. As previously noted, we begin reminded of nature's perennial promise and plenty. "The sun shines to-day also. There is more wool and flax in the fields." Contextually, the "wool and flax" of the present contrast to the "faded wardrobe" of the past. Intertextually, as I've mentioned, the phrase calls up the cluster of associations it has in the Bible. Clothing is the main such reference, but the allusion is richer still. Throughout the Bible, harvest is associated with the fruition of God's promise. In the Gospel of John, the harvest motif and the image of fields whitened with wool and flax are conflated as a sign of messianic

imminence. "Say not ye, There are yet four months, and then
cometh harvest? Behold, I say unto you, Lift up your eyes, and
look on the fields; for they are white already to harvest" (Jn.
4.35). As there is a striking resonance in this passage with the
similar passage of Luke 17 which concludes *Nature,* it would not
be surprising if Emerson had this association in mind. T. S. Eliot
certainly must have when he remarked on a similar and an
unseasonal whitening.

> . . . . This is the spring time
> But not in time's covenant. Now the hedgerow
> Is blanched for an hour with transitory blossom
> Of snow, a bloom more sudden
> Than that of summer, neither budding nor fading,
> Not in the scheme of generation.
> ("Little Gidding," I, 13–18)

In general, and particularly in apocalyptic texts, the whiteness
of wool colors the revelations from above. So in Daniel, "I beheld
till the thrones were placed, and the Ancient of days did sit, whose
garment was white as snow, and the hair of his head like pure
wool; his throne was like the fiery flame, and his wheels as burning fire" (Dan. 7.9).[37] From Mt. Patmos John describes his vision
of the Son of Man in a similar way: "His head and his hair were
white like wool, as white as snow; and his eyes were like a flame
of fire" (Rev. 1.14). Throughout the Bible whiteness is a figure of
righteousness: it is the color which remains after the purification
of sin (Is. 1.18); it is the color of God's raiment. Interestingly, it is
also the color of the bride's linen when she is presented in marriage to the Lamb (Rev. 19.8).

One of the great virtues of whiteness, for Emerson as for the
biblical writers, is its purity. It looks over into transparency. In
Saint John's Revelation this association is clear. He first sees "the
holy city," the "new Jerusalem" (21.2), descending out of heaven as
a bride arrayed in the white linen of righteousness (19.8). In his
next vision, she appears to him as a "great city" whose "light was
like a stone most precious . . . clear as crystal" and whose street
"was pure gold, as it were, transparent glass" (Rev. 21.10ff). Some-

thing of this imagery certainly seems to have conditioned Emerson's own vision of the "city of God" in *Nature* (CW, I, 8–9), but more interesting is the collocation there of winter and transparency. In the Journals he remarked that "snow and moonlight make all landscapes alike" (JMN, IV, 377). This is the generalizing effect of winter; it keeps the whole creation of forms but blends them in a blanket of white. Winter is the last stage, the last stopping-off place, we might say, between this world and the next. For if you proceed one more step in the direction of absolute white, the creation disappears—another step brings Easter and the Sun. For Emerson this was always, it seems, part of the import of winter. It proclaimed the end of the world. At least this is what he seems to hear at the start of "The Snow Storm":

> Announced by all the trumpets of the sky,
> Arrives the snow . . .

Transparency is a theme that turns up frequently in Emerson's writings, perhaps most memorably here in *Nature*. It is meant to convey the full promise of Vision; and, given the obvious preoccupation with eyes and eyesight in these pages, it is natural for critics to examine Emerson's optical theories for further clues to his meaning. But while such investigations may shed some light, they risk the danger of becoming tangential to the main axis of his vision, which, as I have tried to suggest here, is ultimately biblical and not scientific. A full elucidation of Emerson's use of a theme such as transparency depends upon our recognition of how richly and inextricably it participates in a tradition of themes, images, and metaphors whose matrix is the Christian Bible. However displaced from this source his own nineteenth-century usage might be, it is to this linguistic basis that we must return if we are to get a full and accurate sense of the resonance of his words. The words of *Nature* are conditioned after all by the words of Scripture. Even Vision, we should remember, is in the end a biblical figure of speech, and transparency a trope for transcendence.

2 *Kenosis* and Creation

> *The law, the gospel, and the Providence,*
> *Heaven, Hell, the Judgment, and the stores*
> *Immeasurable of Truth and Good*
> *All these thou must find*
> *Within thy single mind*
> *Or never find*
> —"Gnothi Seauton" (JMN, III, 292)

In spite of his claim to the contrary, Emerson does not take his
nature quite at face value. The same may be said of his Bible. He
leans a little in his reading. Taking his lead from the visions of
the Book which are themselves revisions, he habitually reads
from his Bible over into himself. A devoted peruser of the spiritual sense, he carelessly allows the literal readings to gather dust
on the shelf. It is not surprising then that the Revelation he copies
down from the scripture he reads looks little like the original. To
many, in fact, there may be no resemblance at all, but then, as we
shall see later, this depends upon the reader.

Emerson did not start out reading this way; it resulted from a
peculiar kind of education. The main thrust of this education was
centripetal—to inspect, to internalize, to take to the self. It only
followed that, in the end, this is where the apocalypse would come

to be seen. This was the site of Revelation, Emerson realized, here and not in heaven, now and not at the end of historical time. To appreciate then the nature of the Revelation he copied down, it is necessary to consider in some detail the impact of his education on his biblical reading.

Optics and Undulation

Discouraged or thrown off the track by Emerson's displacement strategies, many critics have looked elsewhere than *Nature*'s textual foundations for the key to turn the locks to its culminating apocalypse. Barbara Packer locates that key in this sentence, "The axis of vision is not coincident with the axis of things, and so they appear not transparent but opake," which for her is the most important sentence in the book, since it suggests Emerson's conception of the mechanics of the Orphic apocalypse (CW, I, 43).[1] She traces the axis-of-vision formula to a life of Newton he had been reading in the early thirties that was written by the English astronomer David Brewster and published in 1831. Chapter 6 of Brewster's book discusses Newton's hypothesis that light propagates according to a principle of undulation and moves in "fits of easy transmission and reflexion," while the following chapter introduces the subjects of transparence and opacity. Combined with ideas Emerson may have gotten from Reed and Coleridge, this understanding of the mechanics of the propagation of light suggested that the explanation for man's divorce and alienation from nature may actually be laid to imperfect vision. For when the axis of the eye perfectly parallels the axis of the world, then according to this view the world becomes transparent.

Brewster's gloss on Newton's *Opticks* provided Emerson with a figure which made a welcome addition to his collection of ways to overcome the schism between mind and matter. In 1833 he cited Newton's "law of light" as the natural counterpart to the fluctuating inspirations of the soul (JMN, IV, 87), and a couple of months later he noted that "to an instructed eye the universe is transpar-

ent. The light of higher laws than its own shines through it"
(JMN, IV, 96). The more he thought about it, the more the law of
"Undulation"—Newton's "fits"—seemed to explain. By the time
he was at work on "The American Scholar," it had become an
indispensable principle of adhesion, a kind of glue of the universe,
binding together all the oppositions in the matrix of time and
space. Combined with the principle of Polarity, it held out great
promise as nothing less than a universal theory of nature.

> The great principle of Undulation in nature, that shows
> itself in the inspiring and expiring of the breath; in desire
> and satiety; in the ebb and flow of the sea, in day and night,
> in heat and cold, and yet more deeply ingrained in every
> atom and every fluid, is known to us under the name of
> Polarity,—these "fits of easy transmission and reflection,"
> as Newton called them, are the law of nature because they
> are the law of spirit. (CW, I, 61)

As Stephen Whicher and Sherman Paul compellingly established long ago, the principle of Polarity served as the keystone of
Emerson's cosmological vision. The conception of a hierarchical
structure constituted of interlinking axes of polarity provided him
with a scaffolding upon which he could hang the whole continuum
of existence. The one and the many, faith and experience, freedom
and fate, reason and understanding—even these abstract subjective values could be easily accommodated within this vision.[2]

Although the conception of Polarity does not seem to have arrived at full-blown maturity until the late thirties, it has deep roots
in Emerson's earliest expressions of his cherished doctrine of Compensation. In the opening entry of his "Wide World" journal of
1822, Emerson had devoted several paragraphs to a law of "Contrast" which has obvious affinities with the later conception of
Polarity: "Contrast is a law which seems to exist not only in the
human mind with regard to the objects of imagination as an associ-
ating principle but also to obtain in the course of providence and
the laws which regulate the World. When the day grows very
bright and the atmosphere burns with unusual splendour, the
mind reverts to the storm which will cloud, or the night which will

speedily blacken it" (JMN, I, 60). As this early passage suggests, it is the ethical doctrine of Compensation that fires Emerson's vision of Polarity. So it is not surprising that we meet with the clearest formulation of that vision in his essay titled "Compensation":

> Polarity, or action and reaction, we meet in every part of nature; in darkness and light; in heat and cold; in the ebb and flow of waters; in male and female; in the inspiration and expiration of plants and animals; in the equation of quantity and quality in the fluids of the animal body; in the systole and diastole of the heart; in the undulations of fluids, and of sound; in the centrifugal and centripetal gravity; . . . An inevitable dualism bisects nature, so that each thing is a half, and suggests another thing to make it whole; as spirit, matter; man, woman; odd, even; subjective, objective; in, out; upper, under; motion, rest; yea, nay. (CW, II, 57)

While the ethical coloring of this doctrine derives from Emerson's own views on Compensation, it owes its scientific phrasing to Coleridge. In *The Friend,* a book Emerson was perusing in 1829, Coleridge had written that the phenomenon of electricity was but one expression of "a law which reigns throughout all nature, the law of Polarity."[3]

More important for our purposes here, however, is another of Coleridge's formulations which seems to have made a deep impression on Emerson's conception of the mind. In Chapter 12 of the *Biographia* Coleridge posits that intelligence should be conceived as a self-generating, "indestructible power" constituted of "two opposite and counteracting forces, which, by a metaphor borrowed from astronomy, we may call the centrifugal and centripetal forces. The intelligence in the one tends to *objectivize* itself, and in the other to *know* itself in the object."[4] In the famous chapter on the imagination, he adds: "grant me a nature having two contrary forces, the one of which tends to expand infinitely, while the other strives to apprehend or *find* itself on this infinity, and I will cause the world of intelligences with the whole system of their representations to rise up before you."[5] Though in a less inspired vein,

Emerson echoes Coleridge's idea in, among other places, his essay "Politics." "The fact of two poles, of two forces, centripetal and centrifugal, is universal, and each force by its own activity develops the other" (CW, III, 124). Here Emerson borrows from Coleridge in moving toward his own conception of one law of nature that underlies all the rest. So, for instance, in his later essay entitled "Nature," he writes that "motion or change, and identity or rest, are the first and second secrets of nature: Motion and Rest. The whole code of her laws may be written on the thumbnail, or the signet of a ring" (CW, III, 105). What is provocative for Emerson about the Englishman's somewhat abstruse doctrines is not so much the polarities they postulate as their sense of an oscillating and compensatory current which runs between the poles. It is the *relationship* the poles define that intrigues Emerson, and not the mere fact of their opposition. And, as for Coleridge, the vital application of the theory is not to natural phenomena so much as to human experience. By the end of 1835, he had synthesized the various elements of the theory and was proposing it as an explanation for all spiritual progress:

> There are two objects between which the mind vibrates like a pendulum; one, the desire of truth; the other, the desire of Repose. He in whom the love of Repose predominates, will accept the first creed he meets, Arianism, Calvinism, Socinianism; he gets rest and reputation; but he shuts the door of Truth. He in whom the love of Truth predominates will keep himself aloof from all moorings and afloat. He will abstain from dogmatism and recognize all the opposite negations between which as walls his being is swung. (JMN, V, 112)

Consistent with his growing advocacy of an untrammeled freedom in all matters pertaining to religion, Emerson leans heavily away from the repose side of the pendulum, even though the metaphor as such suggests balance. By replacing it with the figure of a self-generating, self-transcending circle, Emerson was able to grant his religious creed the authority of a law of spiritual growth. The classic formulation is in "Circles."

The life of man is a self-evolving circle, which, from a ring imperceptibly small, rushes on all sides outwards to new and larger circles, and that without end. The extent to which this generation of circles, wheel without wheel will go, depends on the force or truth of the individual soul. For, it is the inert effort of each thought having formed itself into a circular wave of circumstance,—as, for instance, an empire, rules of an art, a local usage, a religious rite,—to heap itself on that ridge, and to solidify, and hem in the life. But if the soul is quick and strong, it bursts over that boundary on all sides, and expands another orbit on the great deep, which also runs up into a high wave, with attempt again to stop and to bind. But the heart refuses to be imprisoned; in its first and narrowest pulses, it already tends outward with a vast force, and to immense and innumerable expansions. (CW, II, 180–81)[6]

While this penetrating passage, itself suggesting the power of vision, epitomizes more sharply than anywhere else the terrific centrifugation of Emerson's thought, it does not give us the key to it. We are left depending for our revelations on "the force or truth of the individual soul."

The idea has grown up in much Emerson criticism that Emerson's scientific browsings furnish the explanation for much that is recondite in his thought after the watershed of *Nature*. It is commonly assumed that with his resignation from the ministry Emerson increasingly placed his thought on secular, even scientific, grounds and not on his former religious ones. The editors of the *Early Lectures,* for example, comment that Emerson's interest in science "was perhaps the principal agent in his shift from a theological to a secular base for his moral philosophy" (EL, I, 1). Without getting bogged down in a futile quibble over the line of demarcation between science and theology, a very elusive one, I would like to suggest that this alleged shift is actually based on hearsay. It never took place. What is fashioned as a shift in values was really only a change in vocabulary, Emerson being very fond of such changes. In fact, Emerson hardly learned anything from the Book of Nature he had not already got from the Book of Revela-

tion or his own musings upon it. Generally speaking, what he got
from nature was not explanation but analogy—the language in
which he dressed his revelations. Thus, when in the passage from
"The American Scholar" cited above, he first expounds upon the
"great principle of Undulation in nature," he concludes that
"these 'fits of easy transmission and reflection', as Newton called
them, are the law of nature *because they are the law of spirit*"
(CW, I, 61; my emphasis). And in his first mention of Newton's
law of light in 1833, he invokes it not as an explanation but as an
illustration of the periodicity of mysticism: "As the law of light is
fits of easy transmission and reflexion such is also the soul's law.
She is only superior at intervals to pain, to fear, to temptation,
only in raptures unites herself to God" (JMN, IV, 87). The image
of a coincidence of axes that Barbara Packer elucidates is not a
scientific discovery but a way of figuring man's redemption and
fall, as her overall thesis goes to show. Packer's discussion of the
axis-of-vision passage helps greatly to advance knowledge of Emerson's optics and the centrality of it to his figuration, but it is
questionable whether it substantially advances our basic understanding of *Nature*. Practically speaking, what would it mean,
after all, to set the "axes" of vision and world in parallel? How
might one proceed? If this "formula" is a key to *Nature*'s apocalypse, it creates more puzzles than it solves. On closer analysis
the formula is not so much an explanation—either optical or
epistemological—as a metaphor. Perhaps indeed, it is just another of Emerson's scientific feints.

The purpose of science, we have to remember, is to chase nature
down. But in spite of his eclectic reading over various branches of
scientific study, Emerson never fully imbibed the spirit of its
optimism. "The fable of Proteus has a cordial truth," he thought
(CW, I, 27). In fact, Proteus is quite a ubiquitous figure in Emerson's journals. In spite of the caricature of Emerson as one of
America's original Nature-worshippers, an armchair advocate of
the great out-of-doors, there is nothing particularly trusting in
Emerson's attitude to nature. On the contrary, there is a certain
wariness here, even perhaps a little cynicism: "there is throughout nature something mocking, something that leads us on and
on, but arrives nowhere, keeps no faith with us. All promise out-

runs the performance. We live in a system of approximations. Every end is prospective of some other end, which is also temporary; a round and final success nowhere. We are encamped in nature, not domesticated" (CW, III, 110).

While the tone of this passage from the later essay "Nature" varies from that of the 1836 treatment, its vision of nature is of a piece. Nature is a chimera; how can scientific investigation be conducted on such a creature? It is nothing but show, every moment changing. It is elusiveness itself.

> There is in woods and waters a certain enticement and flattery, together with a failure to yield a present satisfaction. This disappointment is felt in every landscape. I have seen the softness and beauty of the summer-clouds floating feathery overhead, enjoying, as it seemed, their height and privilege of motion, whilst yet they appeared not so much the drapery of this place and hour, as forelooking to some pavilions and gardens of festivity beyond. It is an odd jealousy: but the poet finds himself not near enough to his object. The pine-tree, the river, the bank of flowers before him, does not seem to be nature. Nature is still elsewhere. This or this is but outskirt and far-off reflection and echo of the triumph that has passed by, and is now at its glancing splendor and heyday, perchance in the neighboring fields, or, if you stand in the field, then in the adjacent woods. The present object shall give you this sense of stillness that follows a pageant which has just gone by. (CW, III, 111)

In actuality, nature is substantially absent from *Nature*. This partly results from the way it is defined. "Nature," we must remember, is the "Not Me," an appearance only (CW, I, 8). Whatever we can grasp abrogates, by our very grasping, its title to nature. It is our necessary alien, a forever ungraspable. Nature—the nonself—eludes *Nature;* it is *Nature's* surplus of sense. Less even than a Kantian phenomenon, it becomes in Emerson's hands more of an epiphenomenon, the sheerest overtone of circumstances. It is as irrecoverable as the fugitive seashell whose charm evaporates when it is removed from its proximity to the sea.

> The shows of day, the dewy morning, the rainbow, mountains, orchards in blossom, stars, moonlight, shadows in still water, and the like, if too eagerly hunted, become shows merely, and mock us with their unreality. Go out of the house to see the moon, and 'tis mere tinsel; it will not please as when its light shines upon your necessary journey. The beauty that shimmers in the yellow afternoons of October, who ever could clutch it? Go forth to find it, and it is gone: 'tis only a mirage as you look from the windows of diligence. (CW, I, 14)

Technically, Emerson's observation here confines itself to one department of nature only—its beauty—but the journal entry from which it is excavated permits wider generalization:

> I said once that if you go expressly to look at the moon, it becomes tinsel. A party of view hunters will see no divine landscape. There is however in moon gazing something analogous to Newton's fits of easy transmission and reflection. You catch the charm one moment, then it is gone, then it returns to go again. And spoken of it becomes flat enough. Perhaps the "fits" depend on the pulsations of the heart. (JMN, V, 189)

Here in a characteristically Emersonian turn, nature provides only the starting point for a meditation that gravitates back toward the self. It is the first term of a dialectical movement that quickly transcends and, in the process, revises its point of departure. Nature, we might say, is merely the pretext of *Nature*. The moon here is wholly subservient to a book.

In the final analysis, science leads us too far afield. It helps us identify some of the exotic fruits of Emerson's *Nature*, but it leaves the basic structures unanalyzed. For that we need to dig a little into *Nature*'s past, trace its roots in the formative periods of

Emerson's thought. Here and not in science are the elements we need to bring *Nature*'s fuller relevance to light. Emerson himself points us in the direction we are taking—"The golden key / Which opes the palace of eternity," he says, is, after all, just a little old-fashioned "virtue" (CW, I, 38).

The Day of Judgment

Any archaeological handling of Emerson's thought must sooner or later run up against the doctrine of Compensation. It was a creed that served him long and early, and it set the basic terms for all later developments in his thought. In a letter to his brother Edward dated August 15, 1831, Emerson wrote: "That word *Compensations* is one of the watchwords of my spiritual world—and time and chance and sorrow and hope do not by their revelations abate my curiosity" (L, I, 330). But even as early as his college days Emerson looked to belief in an immutable moral law as the wellspring of his faith. When the authority of the Bible began to crumble under the weight of the higher criticism, Emerson was relatively undisturbed, convinced as he was that the essence of Christianity was not in its accounts of the supernatural, but in its advocacy of the moral principal. While studying Divinity Emerson remarked in the margin of his Bible, "What is the reward of virtue? Virtue. This is the sum of Christianity," and in another place, "I esteem it more to the purpose of a true exposition, more in unison with the spirit of Christ, to draw a moral, than to prove a miracle."[7] Two years before the publication of *Nature,* he was just as uncompromising: "It is the distinction of Christianity, that it is moral. All that is personal in it is nought. When anyone comes who speaks with better insight into moral nature he will be the new gospel; miracle or not, inspired or uninspired, he will be the Christ" (JMN, IV, 383). And in *Nature* itself he would still insist: "The moral law lies at the centre of nature and radiates to the circumference. It is the pith and marrow of every substance, every relation, and every process" (CW, I, 26). Whether marshaled for a defense against Hume or the higher criticism, the moral law was Emerson's bulwark against doubt. Though it adjusted itself to the shifting light of his vision, early and late it remained the ground of an unshakable faith.

The centrality of the doctrine of Compensation to Emerson's thought is a commonplace of Emerson criticism. What has not been sufficiently brought out is the fact that this doctrine has its origins in a distinctly religious sensibility that we can only describe as apocalyptic. Emerson's Compensation was not the moral doctrine of secular humanism it turned into. Everywhere in his early writings the moral law appears in the context of an expectation of judgment, and this has its roots in Christian millennialism and the Book of Revelation. In a journal entry of 1832 whose expressions prefigure those found in "Circles," Emerson summarizes instances of compensation in nature and then remarks: "But these are far off signs of compensation. Before tea I counted not myself worth a brass farthing and now I am filled with thoughts and pleasures and am as strong and infinite as an angel. So when one of these days I see this body going to ruin like an old cottage I will remember that after the ruin the resurrection is sure" (JMN, IV, 34). In the first extended passage of the journals, the first "Wide World" of 1820, Emerson begins by speculating on the vastness of space as laid bare by astronomy but then pauses to consider "what is to occur when the wheels shall stop and the wings fall in the immediate presence of the source of light to which for ages past and ages to come they have been and will be advancing." The catalyst for this burst of inspiration seems to have been an oration of Everett which had swelled with apocalyptic imagery, an excerpt of which Emerson copies down. Modulating then to a panegyric on eloquence in general, Emerson goes on to remark that "one of the most grand subjects which the Christian religion contains is the judgment and the noblest theme for eloquence." Rapt in his vision of a procession of generations coming down "to the stupendous tribunal of inexorable Justice," he proclaims, "yes they shall come and their righteousness and unrighteousness, their glory and degradation, their sin and their sacrifice, yea all that they have done shall come with them to judgement." At this point he loses himself in a glut of apocalyptic imagery: "The heavens and all their host are rolled together as a scroll—they are folded up and changed; the world is blazing beneath them and its flame is ascending forever and ever; . . . All all is vanishing but the throne of the everlasting" (JMN, I, 3–9).

In the journals of 1822 we are provided with an entry more characteristic of Emerson's maturer formulations, but here too the moral law is seen in the context of a future judgment: "the moral sense has a divine origin, if anything in man is divine;—because it has a distinct superiority over every other faculty; because it constitutes more of one's self than any other attribute, . . . because it seems to anticipate the future Judgement" (JMN, II, 11).

When reading over Emerson's earliest journals, the ones he called his "Wide World," it is hard not to be struck, and a little surprised, by the prevalence of doomsday rhetoric one encounters there. New England had come a long way since the days of the Great Awakening, but this is difficult to tell from these journals. The sermons he was hearing were evidently still filled with echoes of the old apocalyptic themes, if not exactly fire and brimstone. During the month of December in 1820, he seems to have been nearly obsessed with his visions of the end of time. He recorded one entry that begins, "The human soul, the world, the universe are labouring on to their magnificent consummation," and ends with this excited exhortation:

> Roll on then thou stupendous Universe in sublime incomprehensible solitude, in an unbeheld but sure path. The finger of God is pointing out your way. And when ages shall have elapsed and time is no more, while the stars shall fall from heaven and the Sun become darkness and the Moon blood, human intellect purified and sublimed shall mount from perfection to perfection of unmeasured and ineffable enjoyment of knowledge and glory.

A few days later, Emerson began another entry with the comment: "I am going to set apart a page or two of this variety-shop for unconnected reflections or allusions to the day of retribution to the human race. Teeming with such importance so universal and so intense, it cannot be named too often or pressed with too much force." The heading of the long entry which follows is simply "The Day of Judgement" (JMN, I, 46–48). In the "Wide World" journal of 1822 we are presented with an entry which has a direct bearing on *Nature:* "Without, there is an Order of the Universe—broken, if the Arm which sustains it be withdrawn; and the forerunner of this dissolution, the Angel of Prophecy has already published the day.—Watch, for the Time is at hand—when the heavens shall be rolled together as a scroll and the elements shall melt with fervent heat. What then is Nature?—it is the transitory pleasure of the Divine Mind" (JMN, I, 81).[8]

It is fairly clear that the person principally responsible for nursing Waldo to this feverish apocalyptic pitch was his aunt, Mary Moody Emerson.[9] In a eulogy delivered in 1869, six years after her death, Emerson described with veneration and some humor his aunt's hard, lonely, and at times eccentric life. It was, he said, a "representative life"—one distinguished above all by the passion of her religious genius. To her more than anyone else, he owed his earliest lessons in fortitude, humility, and prayer. The single-mindedness of her own preoccupation with death and the world beyond is evidenced in his facetious recounting of how, as old age approached, she took to wearing her burial shroud as a robe (W, X, 371–404). But the fervency and perseverance of her conservative religious feeling and the high esteem in which she was held by her nephews suggest that such practices could not be dismissed as symptoms of religious pathology. As Stephen Whicher aptly puts it, she showed Emerson "something of the white-hot core of the original Calvinistic piety."[10]

For the young Emerson there seems to have been no influence as consequential as that of Mary Moody Emerson. She was his earliest and, for long stretches of time, his primary correspondent and mentor. He studiously copied long extracts of her letters into his journals. The standard view is that she was mainly Emerson's representative apologist for the old Calvinist faith. She was partly this, but as Phyllis Cole suggests, she was also young Emerson's co-explorer in the area of new ideas and perhaps at times even the main instigator of some of the centrifugal tendencies which, in the end, would lead to apostasy and his irreconcilable break with organized religion and with her.[11] In any case, there can be no doubt of the love and admiration he felt for his charismatic aunt:

> The religion of my Aunt is the purest and most sublime of any I can conceive. It appears to be based on broad and deep and remote principles of expediency and adequateness to an end—principles which few can comprehend and fewer feel. It labours to reconcile the apparent insignificancy of the field to the surpassing grandeur of the Operator and founds the benignity and Mercy of the Scheme on adventurous but probable comparisons of the Condition of other orders of being. Although it is an intellectual offspring of beauty and splendour, if that were all, it breathes a practical spirit of rigid and austere devotion. It is independent of forms and ceremonies and its ethereal nature gives a glow of soul to her whole life. She is the Weird-woman of her religion and conceives herself always bound to walk in narrow but exalted paths which lead onward to interminable regions of rapturous and sublime glory. (JMN, I, 49)

Though Mary may have unwittingly conspired with the enemies that would soon bring her age to an end, when she did recognize in Transcendentalism a monster she had helped breed, she quickly showed her true diehard loyalties. What she despised most about the new views her nephew was falling prey to was that they had foolishly left out the Judgment Day and the "consummation of this passing world."[12] But throughout her long correspondence with Waldo, and especially during the period of the early twenties, her letters are rife with allusions to apocalypse and the Book of Revelation. "Ask the Genius assigned to some incalculable period of time, if he does not foresee the moment when the whole history of this world will pass through the hand of some ancient librarian of Heaven as a scroll!" (transcribed in JMN, I, 199). The most suggestive bit of evidence for Mary's influence on Emerson's apocalyptic leanings comes in a retrospective entry he made in his journal in 1837:

I cannot hear the young men whose theological instruction is exclusively owed to Cambridge and to public institution, without feeling how much happier was my star which rained on me influences of ancestral religion. The depth of the religious sentiment which I knew in my Aunt Mary imbuing all her genius and derived to her from such hoarded family traditions, from so many godly lives and godly deaths of sainted kindred at Concord, Malden, York, was itself a culture, an education. . . . In my childhood Aunt Mary herself wrote the prayers which first my brother William and when he went to college I read aloud morning and evening at the family devotions, and they still sound in my ear with their prophetic and apocalyptic ejaculations. Religion was her occupation, and when years after, I came to write sermons for my own church I could not find any examples or treasuries of piety so high-toned, so profound, or promising such rich influence as my remembrances of her conversation and letters. (JMN, V, 323–24)

Though Mary was undoubtedly the main conduit for the apocalypticism of the ferocious old faith, she was probably not the only one. Dr. Ezra Ripley, Emerson's stepgrandfather and Mary's stepfather, was a latter-day paragon of New England's old-time religion. Crotchety, conservative, and sometimes disagreeable as he may have been, he cannot have failed to leave a sharp impression on the younger Emersons. And one of the few entrances he makes into the journals suggests the kind of impression it was: " 'Overturn, Overturn, and overturn,' said our aged priest, 'until he whose right it is to reign, shall come into his Kingdom' " (JMN, IV, 384). Following this brief entry of 1834, Emerson, writing apparently from the Old Manse, hears in the great storm-lashed willow tree over his roof "the trumpet and accompaniment of the storm."

The earliest evidences of Emerson's apocalypticism suggest that at least through his college years he still adhered to a belief in the literal truth of the prophecies of Saint John of Patmos. He was undoubtedly learning to tap these for their rhetorical power as well, as Edward Everett, for one, was evidently doing to such effect. But whatever else the apocalypse had come to signify for Emerson, it was still the eschatological event. The Bible's climactic drama, it would take place at the end of history, and its stage would be the physical world. By the early twenties, however, Emerson's increasing fascination with the moral law began to temper such historicism. As previously suggested, this preoccupation was partly a defensive maneuver, since historical Christianity was showing signs of buckling under the pressures of the higher criticism. But whatever the motivation, for faith the moral law provided an impregnable position. Its seat was to be located in the human conscience, secure from all blasts of circumstance. This shift of perspective did not result in an abandonment of the biblical revelation, since the concepts of judgment and retribution—compensation, in short—were indispensable to it. What it meant was that the whole baggage, minus only the chronological framework, would be transported within. Here were the Rock and the Kingdom. While the full implications of this move within would take some years to unfurl themselves, the new perspective is apparent already in the journals of 1823.

> Now the eternity of physical nature is but a metaphor of speech; an occasional comparison between the longevity of nature and man's momentary life. For in fact the whole period of the material universe may be but a span of time considered in relation to the existence of mind.... But there is no waste no period to the Moral Universe. An antiquity that is without beginning and a futurity that is without end is its history. A principle of life and truth in itself which it is impossible to conceive of, as liable to death or suspension, or as less than infinite in the extent of its rule, binding God and man in its irreversible decree,—is coexistent with Deity.... Quit then your tenacious hold upon the gay world without to make closer acquaintance with the world within. Extinguish the Sun. Annihilate this solid fabric of earth. Forget the forms of life and beauty which adorned it. What is any worth? What are all worth that they should detain the soul a moment from studying the

secrets of that universal and immortal Kingdom which alone will survive this fair and perishable World. (JMN, II, 130)

The oblique allusion here to the blackening of the sun in the memorable passage from Revelation 6.12 and the general apocalyptic tenor of the end of the citation suggest the biblical debt here. For Emerson virtue at no time settled into the complacency of a secular merit. It is charged, always in his imagination and frequently in his expression, with apocalyptic consequences. Typical of this habitual association of virtue and the imagery of apocalypse is this 1834 entry: "Excite the soul and it becomes suddenly virtuous. . . . Excite the soul, and the weather and the town and your condition in the world all disappear, the world itself loses its solidity, nothing remains but the soul and the Divine Presence in which it lives" (JMN, IV, 383).

Essential to Emerson's earliest understandings of Compensation was the belief in future retribution, and the biblical account of that retribution was obviously the governing expression of it. But it was not long before Emerson had begun to subscribe to a theory of instantaneous retribution. In the first sermon he ever gave, "Pray without Ceasing," Emerson insisted that a divine system of judgment operates upon man in each moment of his life whether he knows it or not (YES, 1–12).[13] If, as it seems, Emerson was increasingly inclined to jettison the whole eschatological framework of Revelation, it is a little surprising that we should still be presented with eulogies of the moral law from later writings which are characteristically and habitually tied to apocalyptic imagery and themes. As many of the foregoing passages suggest, the one theme that Emerson particularly favored, both in the early quasi-biblical apocalypses and in the later displaced ones, is that of the dissolution or transparency of the world. This fact points to a deeper and much more vital connection in Emerson's thought between apocalypse and the moral law than has been generally recognized. Retribution only defines the outer connection—the essential connection between the moral law and the drama of the biblical apocalypse has to do with the value of emptiness in the Christian life.

"He Made Himself of No Reputation"

One clue to what I am getting at here comes to us from the passage of 1823 cited above: "Quit then your tenacious hold upon the gay world. . . . Forget the forms of life and beauty which adorned it. . . ." The best gloss of this passage and others like it is the Book of Ecclesiastes—"Vanity of vanities, saith the Preacher, vanity of vanities; all is vanity" (Eccles. 1.2). Etymologically, "vanity" means emptiness. And it is the most pointed way of describing the doctrinally correct Christian's attitude to the physical world. Relative to the Kingdom of Heaven, it is transiency, a mere vanity. We are sojourners in this world only (cf. Phil. 3.20; Heb. 11.15). For the discerning, it is a veil of tears ready to evaporate at the first glance of the Sun's rays. We do not belong to it and it does not belong to us. This is to suggest that the vision of the world as a mere shadow of the eternal leads to a prescription for living, a gospel prescription. Here a second clue comes in. In 1820 Emerson copied into his journal an abstract of a sermon on charity he had just heard Edward Everett preach. The abstract begins with the observation that "the most recommended virtue in the New Testament is *charity*" and goes on to analyze "the great principle" in terms of "1. Love to God and 2. Love to men." For Everett, Emerson, and other Unitarians of their persuasion, the Great Commandment was still the heart and keystone of the moral law. It stemmed from the fact that we are God's people and have nothing in this world which is our own. "*We* must be charitable as the dispensers of his bounty. Our wealth and our wisdom is not our own." And, if this state of affairs is not so evident now, it soon will be (JMN, 44–45).

In this abstract, as in other passages noted above, the discussion of morality is placed under the shadow of Judgment, but the identification of the essence of morality as love or giving suggests that the real link is the implied parallel between denial of self and dissolution of world. Just as in the old historical and eschatological perspective the Revelation of Christ had to await the destruction of the world, so in this revised perspective it was the self that stood between the seeker and the moral kingdom within. In either view some dismantling of the status quo was necessary. For the former it was the whole earth; for the latter it was the sins of selfishness; but in other respects the two perspectives were exactly parallel. In Emerson's imagination, the themes and images of the Book of Revelation informed his expressions of the workings of the moral law, while the hectic excitement of old-fashioned apocalypticism infused his piety of self-denial, giving it an authority and an urgency it would otherwise have lacked. Although the dates had changed, it was still the case that annihilation led to the revelation of God's Kingdom.

Christianity lacks any exclusive claim to religious self-denial, but no virtue was so deeply stamped into the religion Christ inspired than the self-denial of which he is the paragon. The name for it in theology is *kenosis,* and the basic text is Philippians 2.7: "But [he] made himself of no reputation, and took upon him the form of a servant, and was made in the likeness of men." This was a biblical passage Emerson knew well: he quotes it twice in his journals of 1834, and after the second entry he remarks of the statement "He made himself of no reputation" that "the words have a divine sound" (JMN, IV, 380, 382). The literal meaning of the phrase he cites is "emptied himself," and this is probably the sense he took from it. Historically, it has been the basis for an influential Christology, but more important, it provides the basic formula for a kind of piety in which Emerson was nurtured.[14] For him as for his forebears, Christ's self-sacrifice was the key to all true piety. In 1836 he transfers it in an interesting way to nature. "The aspect of nature is devout. Like the figure of Jesus, she stands with bended head, and hands folded upon the breast. The happiest man is he who learns from nature the lesson of worship" (CW, I, 37). For his sermon entitled "Self-Culture" Emerson chose his text from Romans 12.1: "I beseech you therefore, brethren, by the mercies of God that ye present your bodies a living sacrifice, holy, acceptable unto God, which is your reasonable service." He ends by exhorting his parishioners: "The way is plain—the work is simple—we are to give ourselves in every moment living sacrifices. We are to give *ourselves,* that is, all that we have. We are to give *ourselves,* that is, the whole of our being, the present as well as the future" (YES, 104).

Paradoxically, it is this piety of self-sacrifice, and not some humanistic value of self-affirmation, that is the crux of Emerson's early conception of "Self-Culture," a conception that clearly adumbrates the more famous doctrine of Self-Reliance. It also underlies his advocacy of solitude and personal asceticism, both early and late. In an extended encomium in the journals of 1825, he characterizes solitude as "a solitary discipline" consisting "of frequent silence, of invariable temperance, of self-withdrawal from free and jocund society, of stated abstractions of the soul from earthly converse." While "it requires much more selfdenial than most men are masters of," it "gives a breathing space, a leisure, out of the influence of dazzling delusions, the pomp, and vanity of this wicked world; because by removing these outer attractions it sends the soul back on himself" (JMN, II, 329). This passage is interesting in that it faces both ways—forward and back. Its use of a phrase like "vanity of this wicked world" suggests its emotional sources in an old Puritan ethic of world-weariness, while its final locution, "sends the soul back on himself," anticipates the doctrine of Self-Reliance. In actual fact, there is always a vein of this old piety of self-denial even after the great apotheosis of the Self. Here, for example, is a passage from the oration he gave at Dartmouth in 1838: "accept the hint of shame, of spiritual emptiness and waste, which true Nature gives you, and retire, and hide; lock the door; shut the shutters; then welcome falls the imprisoning rain,—dear hermitage of nature. Re-collect the spirits. Have solitary prayer and praise. Digest and correct the past experience. Blend it with the new and divine life, and grow with God" (CW, I, 110).

It is apparent from his correspondence that Emerson's conviction in the efficacy of spiritual emptiness, like his apocalyptic leanings, owes a good deal to his Aunt Mary. Not only was she a lifelong exemplar of this ideal, she kneaded it into the hearts of her willing nephews. This much is easy to recognize. What is more interesting, however, is that it may well have been Mary who first illustrated to Waldo that disgust for the world and isolation of the self may have other rewards than the purely spiritual. In the following excerpt from one of her letters, the sensuality of the language is as revealing as its sense.

Could a mind return to its first fortunate seclusion, where
it opened with its own peculiar colours and spread them
out on its own rhymy pallette, with its added stock, and
spread them beneath the cross, what a mercy to the
age! . . . The heroism of morals, the enthusiasm of eloquence, the love of an eternal fame are supernatural enjoy-
ments allotted only to minds which are at once exalted
and melancholy, and wearied and disgusted with everything transitory and bounded. This disposition of mind is
the source of every generous passion and philosophical
discovery. (J, I, 371)

In this curious and rather lovely passage, we are apprised of the
possibility that Mary Moody Emerson's dominant key of doom
could modulate to sunny major. Whether it does depends largely
on the instrument on which it is played. In Waldo it began habitually to modulate that way, and this is a development worth trac-
ing; in brother Charles, on the other hand, Aunt Mary's world-
weariness remained always the dominant mood, even sometimes
to Waldo's chagrin. "C[harles] thinks that it is only by an effort
like a Berserkir a man can work himself up to any interest in any
exertion. All active life seems an amabilis insania ("fond illusion"). And when he has done anything of importance he repents
of it, repents of Virtue as soon as he is alone. Nor can he see any
reason why the world should not burn up tonight. The play has
been over, some time" (JMN, V, 109–10).

When, a few months before the completion of *Nature*, Charles
was carried off quite suddenly by the same disease that had killed
Ellen, Emerson lamented, "The eye is closed that was to see Nature for me, and give me leave to see" (JMN, V, 152). From the
time they were children, but especially in his last years, Charles
was Waldo's closest confidant, friend, interlocutor. After Emerson
had passed out of his aunt's orbit, it was Charles who became the
exemplar of a piety of spiritual emptiness. The allusion in *Nature*
to the "figure of Jesus" cited above owes its inclusion to Charles.
"He thought Christianity the philosophy of suffering; the religion
of pain: that its motto was, 'Thy Will be done'; and that the print
of the bended head of Christ with hands folded on the breast

should be the altar-piece and symbol in churches, and not the crucifixion" (JMN, V, 154).

There is one more influence which needs to be examined if we are to see how Emerson made the passage from Christian self-abnegation to transcendentalist self-affirmation. In a letter of 1835, Emerson wrote to a correspondent, Benjamin Hunt:

> You used to talk of Self-Reverence. That word indeed contains the whole of Philosophy and the whole of Religion. I would gladly know how profoundly you have pierced it. Did you ever meet a *wise Quaker?* They are few, but a sublime class of speculators. They have been perhaps the most explicit teachers of the highest article to which human faith soars the strict union of the willing soul to God and so the souls access at all times to a verdict upon every question which the opinion of all mankind cannot shake and which the opinion of all mankind cannot confirm. (L, I, 433)

As Rusk remarks in his note, this passage is perhaps Emerson's clearest avowal of the connection between the Quaker doctrine of "the inner light" and his developing doctrine of Self-Reliance. It is hard to exaggerate the impact of Quakerism on transcendentalist ideology. A year earlier, when pressed to identify his religious affiliation, Emerson said, "I believe I am more of a Quaker than anything else. I believe in the 'still small voice,' and that voice is Christ within us."[15]

What Quaker ideas helped him to do was temper the starkness of Christian self-denial with a view that found solace in the self. In the Quaker perspective, the empty halls of the self were brightened from within by an unfaltering divine light. This was the faith Emerson needed to rest his rebirth on. One point of light and all his pantheons could be generated. But this view had other adherents besides Quakers. What he seems to find particularly significant in Quakerism was the piety that went along with it. One of his most memorable introductions to Quaker piety seems to have taken place in New Bedford when he made the acquaintance of two Quaker women, Mary Rotch and Deborah Brayton. On one visit there in 1834 he recounts approvingly a long story told him by Miss Rotch illustrating her obedience to the inner voice. He ends the passage by asking himself, "Can you believe, Waldo Emerson, that you may relieve yourself of this perpetual perplexity of choosing? by putting your ear close to the soul, learn always the true way" (JMN, IV, 264). A month later he further records Quakers' testimony, this time originating with one Mary Newhall, who describes the evolution of religion as moving through three stages—from the Mosaic dispensation through "the more spiritual dispensation of our Saviour" to the "yet more inward and spiritual dispensation of the present day." She compares these three dispensations to stages of purity in the human heart: "from loving our neighbor as ourselves to loving our enemies and lastly arriving at that state of humility when self would be totally abandoned and we could only say Lord be merciful to me a sinner" (JMN, IV, 268).

Emerson had been familiar with the ideas of George Fox for some years; in fact, he was reading extensively in William Sewel's history of the Quakers and probably Tuke's *Memoirs of the Life of Fox* when he was contemplating his resignation from the ministry in July of 1832.[16] But these new contacts with Quaker piety seem to have galvanized a renewed interest in him, for by the next year he is researching a lecture on the founder of the Quaker faith. Certain of Fox's doctrines—such as the "law of criticism" which he cites in the "Language" section of *Nature*— made a lasting impression on Emerson. Another is suggested by a particular turn of phrase which Emerson seems to have taken a fancy to. In a journal entry of 1837 he contrasts ostentatious "talk from the memory" with the self-effacing "talk from the moment," and advises: "do not shine but lie low in the Lord's power, wait and follow with endeavoring thoughts the incidents of the conversation, and you shall come away wiser than you went. You shall be uplifted into new perceptions" (JMN, V, 426–27).[17] The phrase "lie low in the Lord's power" belongs to George Fox, but it comes to designate for Emerson an essential principle of higher life. In the context of "Spiritual Laws," an essay of 1841, it comes up again, and here it reflects its full legacy, from Fox and Mary Rotch back to the spiritual emptiness enjoined by Aunt Mary and Emerson's Calvinist forebears: "Be, and not seem. Let us acquiesce. Let us take our bloated nothingness out of the path of the divine circuits. Let us unlearn our wisdom of the world. Let us lie low in the Lord's power, and learn that truth alone makes rich and great" (CW, II, 92–93). Obedience, literally a "listening," is the key to Emerson's "Spiritual Laws," just as it is to Quaker piety.[18] And though the Quaker inner light became in Emerson's vision an all-governing sun, still it would reveal itself only once the ego had withdrawn into waiting and self-forgetfulness. This is true for Emerson early and late. Here, for example, is the way he brings his "Circles" to an end: "The one thing which we seek with insatiable desire, is to forget ourselves, to be surprised out of our propriety, to lose our sempiternal memory, and to do something without knowing how or why; in short, to draw a new circle. Nothing great was ever achieved without enthusiasm. The way of life is wonderful: it is by abandonment" (CW, II, 190). The stronghold of Emerson's imperial Self could never be taken by storm, only by absolute surrender. Purgation was the way to revelation; abandonment was the way to enthusiasm, that is, to the god within.

"God Dwells in Thee"

George Fox was not the first to announce the good news that "God is within us," as Emerson was quick to acknowledge. Traces of this faith, he thought, could be found in Socrates, Homer, and the doctrine of special providence (EL, I, 172). In fact, Fox's belief in the infinitude of the private man was a perennial truth that was, unfortunately, perennially ignored. "All religious movements in history and perhaps all political revolutions founded on claims of Rights, are only new examples of the deep emotion that can agitate a community of unthinking men, when a truth familiar in words, that 'God is within us,' is made for the time a conviction" (EL, I, 181). The familiar words—though this Emerson did not have to say—are a paraphrase of Christ's teaching in Luke 17.21, but it is interesting that here he also connects this teaching with human rights.

In this relatively late discussion of the doctrine of "God within," something of its long background in Emerson's thought may be discerned. This development has been perceptively delineated by Stephen Whicher, so there is no point in going over it again in detail here.[19] As he suggests, the roots of Emerson's exuberant theology of immanence were in his trusted old doctrine of Compensation. It was on his abiding faith in the immutability of moral law that Emerson rested his belief in personal immortality, and it was in his faith in personal immortality that he based his theology of God within. For Emerson this triple foundation was solid and very deep—solid and deep enough, in fact, to support the whole sprawling and ungainly edifice of Self-Reliance, which Emerson founded. For my purposes here, it is enough to emphasize the continuum that runs between Emerson's early piety of God-reliance and his later piety of Self-reliance. He has not collapsed God into self; rather he has founded the self upon God. His revision was not a philosophy of narcissism; it was closer to the old theology, only resituated.[20] This is a point he makes clearly for his congregation, and perhaps for himself, in one of his earliest formulations of Self-Reliance, a sermon he delivered in 1830 called "Trust Yourself":

> Nor on the other hand let it be thought that there is in this self-reliance anything of presumption, anything inconsistent with a spirit of dependence and piety toward God. In listening more intently to our own soul we are not becoming in the ordinary sense more selfish, but are departing farther from what is low and falling back upon truth and upon God. For the whole value of the soul depends on the fact that it contains a divine principle, that it is a house of God, and the voice of the eternal inhabitant may always be heard within it. (YES, 110)

The piety dictated by Self-Reliance will be parallel to that dictated by the old otherworldly religion of self-sacrifice. Two terms remain, God and self, only now represented by the two-tiered structure of higher and lower self; but it is still the case that the path to the former involves the necessary sacrifice of the latter.[21]

Although the idea of divine immanence had stirred Emerson periodically for many years, it seems to have precipitated something akin to religious awakening starting around 1830. Whicher maintains Coleridge was the catalyst. I will suggest something closer to home. But whatever triggered Emerson's enthusiasm, it is generally acknowledged that the first full proclamation of the new faith comes in the gnomic poem "Gnothi Seauton," which Emerson drafted into his journal on July 6, 1831.[22]

> If thou canst bear
> Strong meat of simple truth
> If thou durst my words compare
> With what thou thinkest in the soul's free youth
>
> Then take this fact unto thy soul—
> God dwells in thee.—

As Cameron points out, Emerson addresses the poem to himself, adopting for his revelation the form of an oracle. And the oracle's message, of course, is the same as the famous one from Delphi— "Know thyself." But these debts to Greek religion notwithstanding, the bulk of this unfinished verse has a staunch biblical flavor. It is not enough simply to internalize the great God above; the oracle must internalize the whole biblical corpus: "the law, the gospel, and the Providence, Heaven, Hell, the Judgement, and the stores Immeasurable of Truth and Good." "All these," says the oracle, "thou must find / Within thy single mind / Or never find." The title may be Greek, but the imagery, themes, and mythology are all markedly Judeo-Christian.

Furthermore, a careful reading will show the oracle's reliance on apocalyptic themes and imagery. Daniel, hero of the Hebrew Bible's greatest apocalypse, is the prototypical "wise man" here. And when the revelation comes to be represented, it depends on the imagery of traditional apocalypse to give it body.

Clouded and shrouded there doth sit
The Infinite
Embosomed in a man

.   .   .   .

But if thou listen to his voice
If thou obey the royal thought
It will grow clearer to thine ear
More glorious to thine eye
The clouds will burst that veil him now
And thou shalt see the Lord.

From this point on, the journals witness a regular barrage of
allusions to the God within. More and more frequently, especially
in the months just before and during his first trip to Europe,
Emerson was to find God, and with him the whole future, "in the
bottom of the heart."²³ His visit to the Old World seems in general
to have done much to intensify Emerson's apocalyptic sensibili-
ties. A poem which he drafted into his journals while in Rome
looks forward expectantly to the time when "the hour of heaven
will come, the man appear" (JMN, IV, 71). And just before debark-
ing from Liverpool the following September, he entered this pregnant paraphrase of Romans 8.22–23: "The whole creation groan-
eth until now waiting for that which shall be revealed" (JMN, IV,
85). At this point revelation has become completely internalized,
but it has not in the process lost anything of its dramatic form.
When Emerson conceives the inner revelation, he still does so
with the help of the old apocalyptic vision; nor has he lost anything of the old apocalyptic fervor. By the time he sets foot again
on American soil, his revelation of the God within has him at a
pitch of excitement, and the first sermon he would preach after
his return reflected it: "Man begins to hear a voice in reply that
fills the heavens and the earth, saying, that God is within him,
that *there* is the celestial host. I find that this amazing revelation
of my immediate relation to God, is a solution to all the doubts
that oppressed me" (YES, 200).

As early as 1830 Emerson had made it clear to himself and his
parishioners that the Revelation of Jesus Christ was not to be
confined to particular times and places. Judgment was all-

pervasive and instantaneous. It was coeval with character. "We interpret the Scriptures when they speak of judgment as always referring to God's award upon character after this life, and so are apt to forget that the laws of God are eternal, and, as they have no end, *so they have no beginning*" (YES, 101). In such early formulations Emerson does not differ materially from the view of Jesus' teachings which he expressed in his "Address" to the Divinity School in 1838. As for all true prophets Jesus' concern was with "the eternal revelation of the heart" (CW, I, 81). Revelation was not from above, but from within. It was, he wrote still later, the disclosure of the soul before which "Time, Space, and Nature shrink away." Revelation was "an influx of the Divine mind into our mind," but as we have seen, it was also "an ebb of the individual rivulet before the flowing surges of the sea" (CW, II, 162, 166).

Emerson's readings of Milton, Wordsworth, Coleridge, and others had prepared him for conceiving the apocalypse in psychological terms, but no depiction of the interior revelation had been as flamboyant as Carlyle's. Here is Teufelsdröckh's description of his personal revelation:

> The hot Harmattan wind had raged itself out; its howl went silent within me; and the long-deafened soul could now hear. I paused in my wild wanderings; and sat me down to wait, . . . I seemed to surrender, to renounce utterly, and say: . . . Let me rest here: for I am way-weary and life-weary; I will rest here, were it but to die. . . . Here, then, as I lay in that Centre of Indifference; cast, doubtless by benignant upper Influence, into a healing sleep, the heavy dreams rolled gradually away, and I awoke to a new Heaven and a new Earth. The first preliminary moral Act, Annihilation of Self, had been happily accomplished; and my mind's eyes were now unsealed, and its hands ungyved.[24]

As we can see from this re-creation of revelation in "The Everlasting Yea," Carlyle is as fully convinced as Emerson of the necessity of self-sacrifice. For both, clearance or purification of the individual self was the prerequisite for inner awakening and the basis of morality. For Emerson this awareness of the redemptive and creative value of emptiness became so habitual, and so affirming, that he came to look upon the direst visions of the eschaton with something like cheerfulness, even levity. When a certain Millerite confronted him with news of the end of the world, Emerson replied mildly, "Well, let it go; we can get on just as well without it."[25]

Northrop Frye has remarked that "the apocalypse is the way the world looks after the ego has disappeared."[26] Despite its obligation to a post-Freudian understanding of the mind, Emerson would have no trouble with Frye's formulation. For him as for Christian and post-Christian thinkers throughout the centuries, the prophecy that sees holocaust followed by the creation of the new heaven and earth was the best paradigm for conceiving and expressing any mystical rending. Every illumination was preceded by its dark night; every rebirth must follow spiritual emptiness. The New Testament itself sanctions this internalization of apocalypse when Saint Paul borrows the Old Testament formula: "Therefore, if any man be in Christ, he is a new creation; old things are passed away; behold, all things are become new" (2 Cor. 5.17).[27]

Emerson's droll rejoinder to the Millerite reflects his mature repudiation of all religious claims predicated on a rigid historicism, but his internalization and universalization of revelation did not by any means dilute its human significance. If revelation was the announcement of the soul, the soul was sanctioned by the "divine inmate." For Emerson as for many devoted readers of the King James Bible, the authorization for conceiving revelation this way was to be found in the Gospel of Luke. When Christ "was demanded of the Pharisees, when the Kingdom of God should come, he answered them and said, 'The Kingdom of God cometh not with observation. Neither shall they say, Lo here! Or lo there! For, behold, the Kingdom of God is within you' " (Lk. 17.20–21). This gospel saying, itself a revision of the older Jewish apocalypticism, was one of Emerson's favorite biblical passages, and it was indispensable for his own revelation of the god within.

Up until now I have been discussing emptiness primarily in connection with Emerson's biblical reading, but this does not fully convey the personal significance it had for him. If Emerson's conception of emptiness as holy pregnancy was first suggested by the Book of Revelation and the piety of the Christian saints, it was authenticated for him in his repeated experience of personal loss. In his own life Emerson had several crucial occasions in which to discover the value of emptiness: death bore it in upon him—death of his father, his brothers, his wife, his child. Just as Hawthorne's scarlet letter stands out vividly against a background of black, so Emerson's magisterial productions emerge from a predominant background of loss and repeated death. The wonder is that he had the courage to survive at all, never mind pronounce and create. This at least would be the common view. But a careful reading of Emerson's life suggests not that he created in spite of his losses but that he created in consequence of them. And my interpretation suggests not only the wider religious context for such a response but its mechanics as well.

A question that many of Emerson's biographers have found hard to avoid is what caused or contributed to the great paroxysm of faith which occurred in the summer of 1831 and yielded the enthusiasm of "Gnothi Seauton." Whicher, as I have indicated, thought Coleridge had something to do with it. More recently, commentators have pointed to the intriguing, perhaps even troubling correlations between Emerson's personal losses and his periodic infusions of creativity.

It is noteworthy that the 1831 proclamation of his faith in the god within is preceded directly by a poem, apparently inscribed on the same day, which is fully as brooding as "Gnothi Seauton" is bright. Here the prevailing tone is morbid and fatalistic: "All the great and good / And all the fair / As if in a disdainful mood / Forsake the world, and to the grave repair," and the subject, as it has been frequently throughout the previous months, is Ellen (JMN, III, 289–90). On February 8, 1831, Emerson's young wife died of tuberculosis—the same disease that would later kill his brothers Edward and Charles. Five days later Emerson recorded his first journal entry since her death: "God be merciful to me a sinner and repair this miserable debility in which her death has left my soul" (JMN, III, 226). For many months, from February onward, the journals are scarred with the passages of Emerson's grief. Yet even before the upsurge of religious inspiration in July, his grief is mollified by a mood of acceptance and faith. On the day of Ellen's death, he wrote to his aunt: "My angel is gone to heaven this morning and I am alone in the world and strangely happy" (L, I, 318). In April he confided in his brother Edward: "I do not know whether I have written to you since Ellen left me. Her loss is a universal loss to me. It makes all life little worth and I go backward to her beautiful character for a charm that I might seek in vain thro the world. But faith is strong—her faith stronger than death and the hope of heaven is more distinct to me by the aid of affection such as hers" (L, I, 321).

Even in its blackest hours Emerson's mourning was ready to brighten into sunlight. Desolation and fullness were for him continuous, not opposed, states of experience. He could barely feel the gnaw of emptiness without anticipating a flood of promise. "Travelling," he wrote to Edward in June, "is a sad recreation to one who finds Ellen nowhere yet everywhere" (L, I, 324). When in August Ellen's sister Margaret started on her own consumptive decline, Emerson was writing to Edward again: "Sad sad it will be to me to lose my high minded sister and yet every star that sinks on this rises in the other firmament and makes the vision of that more full of glory and delight—awful and sweet to me" (L, I, 330). It would be difficult to draw the paradox underlying his grief more sharply than this. New life did not overcome death; it grew from its very heart. Vigor and power arose in proportion to the purity of emptiness. Emerson's faith was a metamorphosis oscillating between nowhere and everywhere, nothing and something, emptiness and fullness. For him the invincible movement from death to rebirth was not just a pious article of faith. It inaugurated several of the most creative periods of his life: behind the religious and vocational awakening of the summer of 1831 was the loss of Ellen, behind *Nature* was the loss of Charles, behind "Experience," in some sense, was the death of the five-year-old Waldo.

Pointing out the relation between the death of Ellen and Emerson's religious inspiration of 1831, and the death of Charles in June of 1836 and the "strong assertion" of *Nature* a few months later, James Cox has argued that "there is a sense in which Emerson literally feeds off the death of those around him." Kenneth Burke, Cox, and Barbara Packer have all duly noted this important correlation. Each explains it differently: Burke as a reenactment of the victimage of the tragic hero, Cox as the spiritualization and assimilation of the loved one, and Packer in terms of the defense mechanisms of incorporation and denial.[28] The metaphor Cox looks to for the mechanics of Emerson's reinvigoration is breathing; the model for Packer is one of eating. In fact, there is evidence that in some psycho-spiritual sense the "sacrifice" of Charles made *Nature* possible. And, in a much more material and financial sense, the death of Ellen made Emerson's vocation as a lecturer and essayist possible. For all these scholars Emerson's resurgent inspiration may be fairly explained as a kind of creative parasitism. What they fail to recognize adequately, however, is the significance of the obvious point: it is not the loved one that is the source and generator of Emerson's creative rebirth, but his or her *loss*. Emptiness consequent on death is what is efficacious for Emerson, not some sort of occult psychological sponging.

Such an explanation for Emerson's periodic fits of inspiration turns of course on a radical paradox and may for this reason sound dubious to readers whose views on creativity are determined by psychoanalytic and other such paradigms. But we should be quick to remember that from a traditional Christian perspective—one which in fact governed Emerson's own views of inspiration—such a paradox makes perfect sense. After all, paradoxes like this one beat at the heart of New Testament teaching and shaped the thinking of generations of Americans until only recently. Fullness of life was not, in this perspective, opposed to emptiness, just as life was never insulated from death: they were rather the alternate swings of a pendulum, possible only in relation to each other. To some extent this kind of unified vision may be seen as a matter of religious faith, but given the mortality rate in early nineteenth-century Boston and the frequency of death in Emerson's family and near circle of friends, it was also a matter of fact and, perhaps, a matter of survival. Emerson's inspiration arose, that is, from the reality of his loss and not through some unrelinquished attachment to the newly deceased.

In a prose poem which Emerson probably drafted into his journal
a few weeks before "Gnothi Seauton," he saluted a "day of salvation" which was undoubtedly his own. Here in lines that show
Easter's Passion and Resurrection to be their paradigm, he clearly
envisions the rebirth that is about to result from the months of
depression over Ellen's passing: "The holy day is come to the sad
wanderer from a sad home and he sends up his sighs, for other
cause for other vanities than he mourned yesterday; o rather let
him now repress Heart's anguish and sin's distress And in his soul
this solemn morn Let the son of God be born" (JMN, III, 234). Like
many other passages during this period, this one turns on the
themes of death and resurrection—of Ellen, of Christ, of Emerson
himself. Here Emerson takes into himself the creative emptying,
the *kenosis,* which for him was definitive of Christ's redemptive
work. The power and enthusiasm of Emerson's revelation of the
god within have prompted many scholars to search for some deci-
sive event, some mystical or creative breakthrough, that could
explain it. The journals of the period give no evidence for such an
event, however—only death and darkness. Yet here, ironically, is
where Emerson felt the impulse of new life. This darkness, and
nothing else, was the source of his revelation.

To Emerson the apocalyptic formula was fitting because it depicted a vivid newness, but more important it gave expression to
the difficult periods of grief, vacuity, or aridity that always
seemed to precede the break from within. It was able to accommo-
date not only his sporadic acquaintance with mystical incursions
but also his more habitual experiences of artistic inspiration. The
prophet, after all, was only a poet raised to full stature.

> A prophet waiting for the word of the Lord. Is it the proph-
> et's fault that he waits in vain? Yet how mysterious and
> painful these laws. Always in the precincts—never admit-
> ted; always preparing,—vast machinery—plans of life—
> travelling—studies—the country—solitude—and suddenly
> in any place, in the street, in the chamber will the heaven
> open and the regions of boundless knowledge be revealed;
> as if to show you how thin the veil, how null the circum-
> stances. (JMN, IV, 274)

To claim that Emerson looked to biblical prophecy for his model of poetic inspiration would not be a surprise to any reader of romantic literature—religious inspiration in one form or another generally provided the model for artistic inspiration to the writers and critics of this era. It may be somewhat more novel, however, to add that it was not only prophecy in general that provided Emerson's model of creative inspiration, but one prophecy in particular—the Book of Revelation. Yet this, in effect, was the role Saint John's vision played in Emerson's imagination. Absorbed by him from the biblical atmosphere he breathed, the apocalyptic theme not only provided the pattern for his piety; it also informed his conception of the dynamics and the goal of the creative process.

> To forget for a season the world and its concerns, and to separate the soul for sublime contemplation till it has lost the sense of circumstances and is decking itself in plumage drawn out from the gay wardrobe of Fancy is a recreation and a rapture of which few men can avail themselves. . . . Ordinary men claim the intermittent exercise of this power of beautiful abstraction; but to the souls only of the mightiest is it given to command the disappearance of land and sea, and mankind and things, and they vanish.—Then comes the Enchanter illuminating the glorious visions with hues from heaven, granting thoughts of other worlds gilded with lustre of ravishment and delight. (JMN, I, 33–34)

The turgid and luxurious style of this passage from Emerson's college days does not disguise the apocalyptic paradigm it is based upon. With the passage of time, apocalyptic language becomes increasingly submerged, but Emerson is always convinced that a great poet must prepare himself thoroughly with periods of abstinence and emptiness before the vision of the new creation can dawn.

Emerson's conception of artistic inspiration turns upon the paradox he found dramatized in the Book of Revelation: the new heaven and earth emerged from the world's annihilation; life depends finally upon death. But the spectacular events of end-time depicted in Revelation participate in a central paradox of biblical revelation as a whole. As we have seen, Christ's redemption of mankind results from his voluntary self-abnegation. He takes upon himself the status of the suffering servant and empties himself for the sake of the world. In this act of divine sacrifice he prefigures the apocalyptic circumstances of his Second Coming but also recapitulates the creation of the world "in the beginning." For in the primordial time of Genesis, we remember, "the earth was without form and void." God, that is, created the world out of nothing. He merely speaks it into being: "And God said, Let there be light: and there was light" (Gen. 1.1–3). In the teachings of the Church, this conception of creation out of nothingness came to be framed in terms of the doctrine *creatio ex nihilo*.[29] Theologically, the significance of this doctrine is that it underscores God's absolute freedom of will. Nothing conditions the divine fiat except unconditional love.[30] In this respect the creative and the redemptive acts are the same: both proceed out of a divine self-emptying which is, in its essential nature, an absolute love. When Christ counsels his disciples to deny themselves for the sake of the Kingdom (Mk. 8.35), he is drawing on an existential paradox that lies at the beginning, middle, and end of biblical revelation.

Emerson did not need to look far to find examples and precedents for his belief in the creative efficacy of religious self-denial; his own New England heritage was filled with exemplars. Indeed, Mary Moody Emerson was one, and in this respect also it is not surprising that she had an authoritative say in the matter:

> Those who paint the primitive state of man's creation are sweet poets; those who represent human nature as sublimed by religion are better adapted to our feelings and situation; but those who point the path to the attainment of moral perfection are the guardian angels. But this is no easy poetic task. The lowly vale of penitence and humility must be passed before the mount of vision, the heights of virtue are gained. (transcribed in JMN, I, 333)

This advice Emerson took very seriously. It became for him the key to artistic inspiration because it was the key to revelation. The artist had before him the activity of the Creator of the new heavens and earth. Emerson studied that precedent with care because he was convinced that the poet who learns that lesson well enough himself "turns the world to glass" (CW, III, 12). The result of his meditation was a program, a technique almost, which lies at the heart of his own book of revelation. It is the business of the next chapter to analyze the nature of that revelation.

3 Easting

> *The whole creation groaneth until now wait-*
> *ing for that which shall be revealed.*
> —Journals, 1833 (JMN, IV, 85)

> *Turning back upon my own Nature, I create*
> *again and again this whole multitude of be-*
> *ings, which is powerless by the force of my*
> *Nature.*
> —Bhagavad Gītā 9.8

Books, like temples, have a way of rising up on the ruins of their predecessors, even when subscribing to an antithetical faith. *Nature* has something of this character. Discernible here and there beneath its leaves and spires are the contours of older foundations. But, for the most part, the evidence for *Nature*'s biblical underpinnings strikes us as equivocal or suggestive only. We have seen in chapter 1 some of *Nature*'s indirect debts to biblical themes and imagery; there are direct borrowings and explicit allusions as well. But on the whole, these seem rather ambiguous or attenuated, almost suspiciously so. With the exception of a few scattered phrases, explicit quotations, and illustrative references to persons or stories, most of Emerson's biblical allusions are mere echoes of the original.[1] Mostly it is a question of phrases, some employed intact, some oddly reinvested, including especially the somewhat unorthodox allusions to 1 Corinthians 13 in the exordium and Luke 17.20 in the peroration. The rest is all oblique—words, rhythms, ideas—like faces we remember but cannot recall from where. It is an impression that results from a literary strategy which, borrowing from Northrop Frye, I have referred to as "displacement." By this term Frye signifies "the techniques a writer uses to make his story credible, logically motivated or morally acceptable—lifelike, in short"[2] For Emerson, it was a way to bring the old Revelation up to date—to make it credible, viable, even sacred once again. The Bible which emerged in the wake of the higher criticism was not to the young seminarian the same Bible he knew in grammar school. Literally and traditionally interpreted, it was no longer fully compelling. The ample heaven was now a fixed ground, the place you started from. For Emerson, as for many of his contemporaries, the Bible was ripe for revision.

The new bible, he believed, must be dictated by the new revelation. That revelation, as we have just seen, proceeds from the recognition that God's throne is nowhere if not in the human heart. The old Revelation was not wrong, just misleading. The meaning construed by some as spiritual must now be construed as fundamental. Nothing essential had to be changed. All that was necessary was a simple conversion of perspective, and once that took place the apocalypse would be recognized for what it really was—a law of the human mind.

Nature is the book Emerson wrote about that discovery. It is, we could say, the testament to his revelation. Critics have remarked on this, and a few have recognized the outer parallels between *Nature* and the Book of Revelation. What they have not sufficiently recognized is that revelation is not simply the subject of the book, it is the essence of the book. *Nature* does not only tell the story of a particular revelation or revelations, it enacts the process, occasions the circumstances, of revelation itself. Its body consists in a series of self-referring revelations; at its heart, unfolded with each of its consecutive expressions, is the law that governs them. It is this law—a law of revelation, for Emerson, a law of life—which is the kernel of Emerson's little book.

The End of Nature

In the beginning of *Nature* we find ourselves already fallen somewhere in the middle of time. Emerson catches us looking back and exhorts us to get our proper bearings in "revelation," "insight," and "an original relation to the universe." We pass quickly through the present and then assume what is apparently the dominant attitude here—an eschatological leaning. Prospectively, we inquire, "to what end is nature?" And here the book's prevailing forward movement ostensibly begins. Our inquiry takes us through "Commodity," "Beauty," "Language," "Discipline," and "Idealism," until we arrive at "Spirit." Each of these way stations responds helpfully but tentatively to our query. Each describes one of the several "uses" of nature but postpones the final answer until the climax of nature in "Spirit." There we learn that: "all the uses of nature admit of being summed in one, which yields the activity of man an infinite scope. Through all its kingdoms, to the suburbs and outskirts of things, it is faithful to the cause whence it had its origin. It always speaks of Spirit. It suggests the absolute. It is a perpetual effect. It is a great shadow pointing always to the sun behind us" (CW, I, 37). Nature's ultimate use is one of reference, we might even say deference, since it always points away from itself at the sense which transcends it. Its "ministry" to Spirit is fulfilled when it sacrifices its own reality. Spirit then is both the culmination and the consummation of nature. The "end" of nature is in its own dissolving.

This is the apparent answer to the question that begins the book. Nature ends where the Bible does, in the apocalypse, and moves roughly according to a parallel teleological scheme. Like the Book of Revelation, and much of the Bible as a whole, Emerson's book on nature is preoccupied with the end of things. But the question arises as to where in nature this "end," this apocalypse, takes place. And when? The Bible, at least, has its sacred times and places to chart the apocalypse by. Nature has no such plan. It lacks the appropriate integrity. It is a gigantic urge—insatiable, unrestrained, and promiscuous in every part. Nature spills over all our holy places and turns our calenders into dust. Like Proteus, it refuses to be caught or contained. This is the nature Emerson saw, for instance, when he was playing mock naturalist in his address "The Method of Nature" in 1841. To all questions, he contended, nature has but one response:

> "I grow, I grow." All is nascent, infant. When we are dizzied with the arithmetic of the savant toiling to compute the length of her line, the return of her curve, we are steadied by the perception that a great deal is doing; that all seems just begun; remote aims are in active accomplishment. We can point nowhere to anything final; but tendency appears on all hands: planet, system, constellation, total nature is growing like a field of maize in July; is becoming somewhat else; is in rapid metamorphosis. (CW, I, 126)

The end is a construct which nature only likes to fool with. No sooner do we mark one end than the next instant it becomes to us a new means: "Nothing in nature is exhausted in its first use. When a thing has served an end to the uttermost, it is wholly new for an ulterior service. In God, every end is converted into a new means" (CW, I, 26). Ends are the artifacts of perception, matters of attention only—they disappear with the next glance. A wider view shows that nature "does not exist to any one or to any number of particular ends, but to numberless and endless benefit, that there is in it no private will, no rebel leaf or limb, but the whole is oppressed by one superincumbent tendency" (CW, I, 126–27). All is a giddy metamorphosis. Nature does not end, it changes. It is a system of self-transcendence—a vast, incessant, insistent instrumentality.

If the apocalypse exists in nature, this then is where to find it: not in the end but in the transformation. It burns over the whole from moment to moment. Every blade of grass recapitulates the destruction and the creation. It is not surprising then that in Emerson's book, as in Whitman's, revelation becomes a very democratic sort of vision. Each sentence, chapter, and paragraph helps to represent it. So even though we are invited in the beginning to look ahead, to anticipate the "end," we have to be somewhat circumspect. There is not far to look. Indeed, we are given a hint on how to read "the end" of nature the first time we are exhorted to ask about it. "Every man's condition is a solution in hieroglyphic to those inquiries he would put. He acts it as life, before he apprehends it as truth. In like manner, nature is already, in its forms and tendencies, describing its own design" (CW, I, 7).

If this passage may be taken as an instruction on how to read nature, it is just as crucial to our reading of Emerson's book. Revelation does not wait till the end. It does not wait to be presented in the showcase of "Spirit" or "Prospects." It especially refuses to be fixed in "facts that end in statement." Propositions cannot confine the revelation we seek (CW, I, 37). The true subject and end of *Nature* continuously elude and exceed *Nature*'s static formulations. If they are recoverable at all, it can only be through a rehearsal of *Nature*'s "forms and tendencies."

These considerations alert us to the significance of *Nature*'s "design." The word is appropriately chosen, and Emerson sanctions its full authority here. It comprehends both "structure" and "end," suggesting further that, while the end develops out of the structure, so the structure reveals the end. Besides these two meanings, a third which Emerson's "design" conveys is "use," a word that he habitually conflates with "end." Apocalypse is the *telos* or end of nature, but it is also nature's highest "use," since, as Idealism teaches, "Nature is made to conspire with spirit to emancipate us" (CW, I, 30). By virtue of *Nature*'s "design," therefore, it follows that the continuous rehearsal of nature's end results, at the same time, in the fulfillment of its highest use. *Nature* moves instrumentally; it is efficacious of its own end—the apocalypse—another feature which, in one sense, it holds in common with the Bible or the Word of God.

But most people conceive the Bible as moving toward Revelation sequentially, in a straight line. As we have seen, this is not the way Emerson conceived *Nature:* if it moved toward revelation, it did so by a series of revolutions. The straight line was an error of vision. Since its end is ubiquitous, "Nature can only be conceived as existing to a universal and not to a particular end, to a universe of ends, and not to one,—a work of *ecstasy,* to be represented by a circular movement" (CW, I, 125). The figure of the circle is found throughout Emerson's writings. The reason for this is explained in "Uriel" by the chant of the poet Seyd:

> Line in nature is not found;
> Unit and universe are round.

But the famous essay of 1841 provides the best commentary on Emerson's favorite figure. "The eye is the first circle; the horizon which it forms is the second; and throughout nature this primary figure is repeated without end. It is the highest emblem in the cipher of the world" (CW, II, 179). Emerson compresses much significance into these circles of his, as various commentators have shown.[3] But there is one illustration whose model they suggest which is of particular relevance here. In the prophetic peroration of "The Divinity School Address," he intones:

> I look for the hour when that supreme Beauty, which ravished the souls of those Eastern men, and chiefly of those Hebrews, and through their lips spoke oracles to all time, shall speak in the West also. The Hebrew and Greek Scriptures contain immortal sentences, that have been bread of life to millions. But they have no epical integrity; are fragmentary; are not shown in their order to the intellect. I look for the new Teacher, that shall follow so far those shining laws, that he shall see them come full circle; shall see their rounding complete grace; shall see the world to be the mirror of the soul; shall see the identity of the law of gravitation with purity of heart; and shall show that the Ought, that Duty, is one thing with Science, with Beauty, and with Joy. (CW, I, 92–93)

In this inspired call for a Western scripture, what Emerson particularly singles out for criticism in the old scriptures is their lack
of "epical integrity." It is difficult to know what, practically speaking, he meant by this, but it is clear at least that he feels the old
books lack unity. Depressed but yet visible behind this demand
for "epical integrity" is the outline of the circle which the new
seers must one day envision. Emerson may even be leaning on
one of the meanings of the prefix *epi:* to encircle or surround.
Whatever the case, the passage as a whole suggests that to the
enlightened eye the perfect scripture will reveal itself in the form
of a circular whole.

But what Emerson gleaned from his reading of nature in 1841
prompts us to recommend further revision still. Nature honors
nothing for long. The circle, like any other figure, is subject to
reform. As a static value it has as little chance to survive as any
other. Nature does not present to us some hypostatized "Circle" but
"circular movement." Its revelation, if it has one, is in its perpetual
self-transcendence. Every fruit or flower is merely another foot-
step of inexorable tendency. What Emerson really needed was a
circle that could transcend itself, and this he found in the spiral.

The clearest representation of this governing figure of *Nature*
will be found, of course, in the motto added to the 1849 edition.[4]

> A subtle chain of countless rings
> The next unto the farthest brings;
> The eye reads omens where it goes,
> And speaks all languages the rose;
> And, striving to be man, the worm
> Mounts through all the spires of form.

Emerson could replace the original motto attributed to Plotinus
with this verse of his own composition because it served merely to
articulate the design he had earlier envisioned. In the Journals of
1834 he recorded this observation: "I saw a hawk today wheeling
up to heaven in a spiral flight and every circle becoming less to
the eye till he vanished into the atmosphere. What could be more
in unison with all pure and brilliant images?" (JMN, IV, 281).

In March of 1836, while working toward completion of his book,

Emerson prefigured the structure that he would use to inform it: "Thus through Nature is there a striving upward. Commodity points to a greater good. Beauty is nought until the spiritual element. Language refers to that which is to be said" (JMN, V, 146). This then is the design which "in its forms and tendencies" *Nature* describes. It circulates upward through its uses like a great helix to heaven. But in contrast to certain other representations of the mystical spiral, this one does not wind up to a point. Rather, it begins at a point and widens as it rises. Each of *Nature*'s uses looks ahead (and above) to a further value that will revise and include it: "Commodity" looks to "a farther good," "Beauty" extends to "an ultimate end"; and "Spirit," as we have seen, sums up all into one.[5] Participating in this helical design, each use prefigures and propagates a new use in the form of a circle, which, curving back on itself, revises and reconstitutes the original one into a new whole. But it is the virtue of the self-referring mechanism of the spiral—the circle's self-reliance, we might say—that in revising itself the spiral simultaneously forecasts the further ends it will eventually entail. Emerson may indeed have found illustrations of his figure in the hawk's hallowing flight, but it is easy enough to see that *Nature*'s design also corresponds to the structure of prophetic revision, signaled by the relation of type to anti-type, that we find so pervasive in the Christian Bible. And here also the revisions wind up in Apocalypse.

The Method of Nature

If the body of *Nature* describes a spiral, so in a sense does its spirit, only here Emerson leans on his pregnant designation "progressive." At the start of "Spirit," he stipulates that "it is essential to a true theory of nature and of man, that it should contain somewhat progressive" (CW, I, 36). As Kenneth Cameron pointed out, the term comes from Coleridge, whom Emerson was reading avidly in the late twenties and early thirties.[6] In *The Friend* Coleridge had argued that true "method" must always involve a continuous "progressive transition" which in turn implies some "preconception," and he contrasted this sort of method with "a mere dead arrangement."[7] Emerson approved this progressive sense of method and, as we have seen, conceived his own inquiry in *Nature* according to it. But, in borrowing Coleridge's sense, he added his own elaboration. In a Journal entry of 1831 Emerson finds in Shakespeare's poetry an apt illustration of Coleridge's method of "progressive arrangement," but he goes on to add, "Another thing strikes me in the sonnets, which in their way seem as wonderful as the plays . . . and that is the assimilating power of passion that turns all things to its own nature" (JMN, III, 299). An entry from the beginning of 1836 suggests that this was the sense of Coleridge's term that he especially favored: "A man is a method; a progressive arrangement; a selecting principle gathering his like to him wherever he goes" (JMN, V, 114). The complete elaboration of this recursive idea awaited the composition of "Spiritual Laws," where Emerson adds this sentence to his previous formulation: "He takes only his own, out of the multiplicity that sweeps and circles round him" (CW, II, 84).[8] Here in the context once again of circles, Emerson indicates the fuller significance that *Nature*'s "progressive arrangement" appears to have. Each sweep of *Nature*'s uses recollects itself. It is designedly self-reflective. This is the deeper basis for the marriage motif discussed previously. When the circle winds back upon itself, it completes a reunion, having the value of self-recognition; and from that contact springs further extension. Only here the sexual metaphor sometimes gives way to one of eating, since the spiritual sense of the spiral is inward not outward. The circles constitute a progressive movement of self-recovery, a movement of self-assimilation. "The lover of nature is he whose inward and outward senses are still truly adjusted to each other; . . . His intercourse with heaven and earth, becomes part of his daily food" (CW, I, 9). With its expanding circulations, the self is nourished, ingests the world, becomes "re-insphered" (JMN, V, 19). The result, a kind of world swallowing, is revelation by alimentation; with digestion completed, only vision remains.

> . . . when I see the daybreak, . . . I feel perhaps the pain of an alien world; a world not yet subdued by the thought; or,

> I am cheered by the moist, warm, glittering, budding, melo-
> dious hour, that takes down the narrow walls of my soul,
> and extends its life and pulsation to the very horizon. *That*
> is morning, to cease for a bright hour to be a prisoner of this
> sickly body, and to become as large as nature. (CW, I, 106)

The spiral's distinction is that it conveys an impression of movement within stasis. It appears to move ahead while at the same
time circling back upon its point of origin. It is an interplay of
centripetal and centrifugal forces. Orbital expansion depends
upon a constant reference to the center of the system. The redeeming value of Emerson's progressive method in *Nature* results from
a similar dynamic. From Coleridge's usage he may have gotten
the prospective push of his design, but to this he added a self-
referential pull, so that each apparent development entails a looking back, as it were, to its source. This double movement in *Nature* tends to compromise any claims to actual progress the sequence of chapters appears to make. Nowhere is this seen more
vividly than in the epiphanies that punctuate the sequence.[9] It is
interesting that the most dramatic and, for that reason, the most
famous of these occurs not at the end of *Nature* but at the beginning. I would like to analyze this famous "transparent eyeball"
passage in some detail later, but for now it is enough to remark
that as an instance of revelation it is a hard act to follow. Here we
are presented with the classic formulation of Emerson's revelation, best described perhaps as an apocalypse of the self—"all
mean egotism vanishes. I become a transparent eye-ball. I am
nothing. I see all. The currents of the Universal Being circulate
through me; I am part or particle of God" (CW, I, 10).[10] Just as in
the cosmic apocalypse, where destruction of the world must precede the new creation, so here dissolution of the self precedes the
beatific vision of self in God. While gleams of this original vision
brighten all the epiphanies in its wake, never again do we get the
hierophany with such blank force, or such sharp completion. Here
at the beginning we discover what the self is. It is the be-all and
the end-all, the beginning of Emerson's revelation as well as its
fulfillment, just as in the Book of Revelation Christ is the "Alpha
and Omega, the beginning and the end, the first and the last"

(Rev. 22.13, 1.11). This revelation of the Self is the ground, the point of reference, for all the revelations that follow. Each new cycle of the spiral, each new section of *Nature,* extends the domain of the Self into the world. By the degrees of "Commodity," "Beauty," "Language," and "Discipline," the whole of nature comes to be seen in terms of the Self. What the seer saw happening to himself in the beginning, he now by stages sees happening to the entire creation. The revelation of the world expands with constant reference to the revelation of the self that occurred in "Nature."

The epiphany that occurs in "Beauty" is an epiphany of perception, but it parallels the previous one of the self—it too is oceanic. In "Nature" the seer stood "on the bare ground" and looked into "currents of the Universal Being"; in "Beauty" he stands on "the earth, as a shore" and looks out into a "silent sea." He partakes of "its rapid transformations." The result is dilation and conspiration "with the morning wind" (CW, I, 13). The word "conspire" here suggests that as the seer expands into his vision he breathes with the wind, but it also suggests that his movement into nature is one of upward spiraling.

Another such "fortunate hour" opens to us in "Language," but here the revelation extends even further—"the universe becomes transparent, and the light of higher laws than its own, shines through it" (CW, I, 22). From now on the continued dilation of the seer precipitates a consecutive apocalypse in nature. In "Discipline" it is his knowledge that triggers it: "What noble emotions dilate the mortal as he enters into the counsels of the creation, and feels by knowledge the privilege to *Be!* His insight refines him. The beauty of nature shines in his own breast. Man is greater that he can see this; and the universe less, because Time and Space relations vanish as laws are Known" (CW, I, 25). And in the regions of the higher philosophy the apocalypse begins when "the eye of Reason opens": "If the Reason be stimulated to more earnest vision, outlines and surfaces become transparent, and are no longer seen; causes and spirits are seen through them. The best, the happiest moments in life, are these delicious awakenings of the higher powers, and the reverential withdrawing of nature before its God" (CW, I, 30). In *Nature* this passage is taken over into a quasi-philosophical context, but it is excised from a Journal passage whose context is religious and apocalyptic. "Religion does that for the uncultivated which philosophy does for Berkeley and Viasa;—makes the mountains dance and smoke and disappear before the steadfast gaze of the Reason" (JMN, V, 123).

Nature's culminating apocalypse is described in the song of the Orphic poet. The second part of that song, the context of the naturalized messianic passage which concludes *Nature,* evinces all the outlines of the apocalypse and epitomizes its whole centrifugal progression: "Nature is not fixed but fluid. Spirit alters, moulds, makes it. The immobility or bruteness of nature, is the absence of spirit; to pure spirit, it is fluid, it is volatile, it is obedient. Every spirit builds itself a house, and beyond its house, a world; and beyond its world, a heaven" (CW, I, 44). But the first part of that song, the Orphic myth proper, is just as suggestive of apocalypse, only here obviously the biblical model has been replaced by a classical one.

This passage explains the disharmony of man and nature in terms of the myths of the Primal Man. In Emerson's myth, the Primal Man has been reduced to a particle of his former heroic proportions. But this shrinkage is only one phase of a larger cycle of contraction and expansion that can account not only for man's fall but also for his redemption. Even within the phase of one degradation, smaller cycles suffice to redeem people at least momentarily. Infancy and death, dreaming and waking—these cycles describe the life even of fallen souls. So, "Infancy is the perpetual Messiah, which comes into the arms of fallen men, and pleads with them to return to paradise" (CW, I, 42). While the first part of the Orphic chant seems to dwell on man's degradation, the myth as a whole is designed to help us conceive his restoration. Emerson's myth of the sleeping giant, like the stories of the disguised King, was a way to represent the unrealized Self. Awakening or recognition symbolized self-realization, and this Emerson would typically figure by drawing on themes of the apocalypse: "The generic soul in each individual is a giant overcome with sleep which locks up almost all his senses, and only leaves him a little superficial animation. Once in an age at hearing some deeper voice, he lifts his iron lids, and his eyes straight pierce through all appearances, and his tongue tells what shall be in the latest times: then is he obeyed like a God, but quickly the lids fall, and sleep returns" (JMN, V, 161–62). As R. A. Yoder suggests, the Orphic allusion draws on the mythical fact that Orpheus was capable of taming rocks, trees, and wild beasts through the magic of his song. By conforming all things to himself, he was able to solve the riddle of nature. His concern too was essentially apocalyptic—"to solve and dissolve nature."[11]

Emerson's Rule

To read *Nature* is to involve oneself in the revolutions of its epiphanies. When our submission to its double movement of reflection and creation is perfect, we internalize its revelation and become the center of a new system. Proof of our success will be that we fulfill Nature's final exhortation—we will build a world of our own (CW, I, 45). This is the point of *Nature*. It is to be a transmitter; its spiral acts as a conducting coil: we pass over and the revelation passes to us. Once it does, so far as we are concerned, the whole apparatus may be left behind, for it has fulfilled its purpose. Nothing in our reading of *Nature* is as consequential as this internalization of its revelation. This is the fruit and flower of our reading, and it repays close attention.

In the summer of 1831, as we have seen, Emerson gave shape to his revelation of the God within in the curious hieratic poem of his Journals that he labeled "Gnothi Seauton." It was a revelation that never lost its grip on his convictions, though in his experience it proved decidedly more elusive. For years Emerson had been troubled by the inconstancy of inspiration, its ebb and flow, but especially its ebb—those long periods of spiritual or creative aridity which commonly followed the moments of exaltation.[12] In 1832, a year after the composition of his oracular poem, he vents renewed frustration at the fickleness of the divine.

How hard to command the soul or to solicit the soul. Many of our actions, many of mine are done to solicit the soul. Put away your flesh, put on your faculties. I would think—I would feel. I would be the vehicle of that divine principle that lurks within and of which life has afforded only glimpses enough to assure me of its being. We know little of its laws—but we have observed that a north wind clear cold with its scattered fleet of drifting clouds braced the body and seemed to reflect a similar abyss of spiritual heaven between clouds in our minds; or a brisk conversation moved this mighty deep or a word in a book was made an omen of by the mind and surcharged with meaning or an oration or a south-wind or a college or a cloudy lonely walk—"striking the electric chain wherewith we are darkly bound." And having this experience we strive to avail ourselves of it and propitiate the divine inmate to speak to us again out of clouds and darkness. (JMN, IV, 28)

Emerson had always given a good deal of thought to the mechanics of inspiration, religious and otherwise, but by 1835 he seems to be toying with the thought that perhaps there is more that we can do than just sit dumbly and wait. "What benefit if a rule could be given whereby the mind dreaming amidst the gross fogs of matter, could at any moment east itself and find the Sun" (JMN, V, 275, 38).[13]

At this point Emerson knows of no such "rule," but his conception of "easting" provided an orientation for a whole way of thinking about the mechanics of inspiration that had been developing for many years.[14] Though he never waivered in his faith that authentic inspiration was the work of the "divine inmate," it began to dawn on him that there was a fair amount one could do to prepare the way of his coming, maybe even incite him a little. Even God, after all, abides by the articles of his covenants, or so Emerson's ancestors had taught him. Perhaps even revelation had its particular rule or method of operation.

One obvious place to look for signs of a law so profound would be nature itself. But we have seen how elusive nature is. Emerson's own conclusion sounds exasperated enough: "The method of nature: who could ever analyze it? That rushing stream will not stop to be observed" (CW, I, 124). Nature's method cannot be analyzed because its expressions will not bear repeating. Nature is a resistless torrent, "a perpetual inchoation." It will not stand still long enough to be analyzed. Yet there is something man might learn of himself even from this. "What is nature to him? There is never a beginning, there is never an end to the inexplicable continuity of this web of God, but always circular power returning into itself. Therein it resembles his own spirit, whose beginning, whose ending he never can find—so entire, so boundless" (CW, I, 54). So while on the face of it all is dizzy flux, there is something in all this expressivity that may give us pause (though perhaps this results from a particular style of reading), and that is nature's eternal contact with its inexhaustible power source. "Not the cause," Emerson wrote in 1841, "but an ever novel effect, nature descends always from above. It is unbroken obedience" (CW, I, 124). Nature refers unceasingly to the area of its invisible origin. Were it to cease even for an instant, life would quickly run down, exhaust itself, and die.

It is interesting that when Emerson discusses the "method of nature" in 1841 the word he introduces to convey this feature of nature's functioning is "obedience," a word evidently not drawn from his reading of scientific literature, but rather from human culture, and conditioned for him especially, as we have seen, by his religious education. Nature evinces "unbroken obedience" to its original cause; it "obeys" one "superincumbent tendency" (CW, I, 127). In fact, here and throughout his remarks in "The Method of Nature," Emerson is anxious to point out the bridge back to human experience. This "superincumbent tendency" which nature always inexorably "obeys" he describes as "that redundancy or excess of life which in conscious beings we call *ecstasy*." While, properly speaking, "ecstasy" also is a word from human experience, it turns out, at least in this address, to be the best way to encapsulize nature's method also. "Ecstasy," says Emerson, "is the law and cause of nature" (CW, I, 132). It directs attention "to the whole and not to the parts; to the cause and not to the ends; to the tendency, and not to the act" (CW, I, 131). And it is best described not as a straight line but as "a circular movement" (CW, I, 125).

Emerson's reliance here in his exposition of nature's "method" on such key words as "obedience" and "ecstasy" suggests perhaps more about his way of reading nature than about nature itself. As in his 1836 treatment, it begins to be apparent that the "nature" of the 1841 oration is something of a misrepresentation. The real subject here, as there, is not "nature" but man. Nature does not suggest the laws of ecstasy or obedience, it illustrates them. Nature is not where we realize obedience, though we might discern its reflection there. Ecstasy is a human word, for Emerson a religious word, whose sense he saw multiplying endlessly from its origin in his own consciousness out to the farthest rim of creation. What it means, he knew, is to stand, "ecstasis," outside oneself. For him it was a law of growth, a law of transcending, a law that governed the self's circling saltation. But the key to ecstasy, whether in nature or the human mind, is obedience, not active energy. Every circle propagates from its center. The essential impulse of ecstasy is not projection but reflection, not action but renunciation. It consists of an aggressive abandonment of all previously created forms, expressions, and ends. "The ends are momentary: they are vents for the current of inward life which increases as it is spent. A man's wisdom is to know that all ends are momentary, that the best end must instantly be superseded by a better" (CW, I, 129). What man learns from such discrimination is the value of retiring: forget the expression, return to the source. Once contact is reestablished, creation rebounds, ushering the old world back up to the minute. It is the lesson, in essence, of "Self-Reliance."

> Life only avails, not the having lived. Power ceases in the instant of repose; it resides in the moment of transition from a past to a new state, in the shooting of the gulf, in the darting to an aim. . . . Why then do we prate of self-reliance? Inasmuch as the soul is present, there will be power not confident but agent. To talk of reliance, is a poor external way of speaking. Speak rather of that which relies, because it works and is. Who has more obedience than I, masters me, though he should not raise his finger. Round him I must revolve by the gravitation of spirits. (CW, II, 40)

In *Nature,* as in "Self-Reliance," it is not the particular formulation that matters but the movement. The book's revelation is everywhere recapitulated in its revolutions. What *Nature* teaches is what the book itself enacts. Designedly, *Nature* articulates the movement of its revelation, by continuously curving back on itself. It is not concerned with advancing some claim upon the back of nature or even, for that matter, speculating about the *terra incognita* of spirit—it is concerned essentially with their relationship. *Nature* abides neither in nature nor in spirit, but circulates restlessly between the two. "The best read naturalist who lends an entire and devout attention to truth, will see that there remains much to learn of his relation to the world, and that it is not to be learned by any addition or subtraction or other comparison of known quantities, but is arrived at by untaught sallies of the spirit, by a continual self-recovery, and by entire humility" (CW, I, 39). This sentence contains Emerson's prescription for inspiration, framed to suggest to his reader a little inside advice. Here epitomized we find once again the distinctive double movement that we saw recapitulated in *Nature*'s spiral structure. Only this time, a principle of physics has given way to a principle of mind. Just as the spire of form must return on itself to propagate anew, so the "sallies of the spirit" must be followed by periodic "self-recovery."

Long ago Sherman Paul recognized in this twofold process Emerson's distinctive "angle of vision." "What is life," Emerson wrote in 1870, "but the angle of vision" (W, XII, 9). For Paul this phrase from Emerson's optics functioned as a metaphor for inspiration. Best interpreted inwardly at the level of consciousness, it derived not from science but from "the religious affirmation of compensation."[15] Though most graphically illustrated in moments of inspiration, the double movement of expression and recovery governs all productive activities of the mind. Here is the way Emerson articulates this principle in *Nature.*

> The intellectual and the active powers seem to succeed each other in man, and the exclusive activity of the one, generates the exclusive activity of the other. There is something unfriendly in each to the other, but they are like the alternate periods of feeding and working in animals; each

> prepares and certainly will be followed by the other. . . .
> Nothing divine dies. All good is eternally reproductive. The
> beauty of nature reforms itself in the mind, and not for
> barren contemplation, but for new creation. (CW, I, 16)

Emerson's views of the mind, like all his central ideas, develop
within the framework of Polarity. What fascinated him, however,
was not the identity, location, or capacity of the mind's terminal
poles, but the psychic electromagnetism which held them in tension. Here also it was the relationship, the movement, that was of
most interest. As we have seen, Emerson seems to have found
Coleridge's astronomical metaphor particularly edifying. Like the
heavenly bodies, the mind was governed by two opposing forces,
centrifugal and centripetal. The one tends to expand infinitely; the
other, Coleridge says, "strives to apprehend or *find* itself in this
infinity."[16] In the case of planets. of course, these two forces exert
themselves simultaneously; in the mind they alternate, precipitat-
ing thereby cycles of expansion and contraction. Mind is thus an
oscillating intelligence, a faculty of rhythm. And its daily history
consists of this "alternating of expansions and contractions" (W,
XII, 53). By easy mechanical analogy, the centrifugal phase of
mind is the phase of creative expression. This is the phase the poet
places at such premium. It is a blaze of glory, but, as Emerson
realized, it is glory that conceals decay, like the autumn foliage
that portends winter. Its energy is kinetic, quickly spending itself
out. To be sustained, it must be recharged. The basis of the mind's
creative expansion, its outward "sallies," therefore, is its contraction. It must continually draw itself back to its source. For Coleridge the mind's centripetal phase culminated in self-knowledge—
mind realizing itself in the midst of its creations. Knowledge is
always centripetal, reflective, temporarily counteracting the outward thrust of creativity. Yet without this resubstantiation of itself, mind cannot continue to create. It is only when mind recollects
and recovers itself in knowledge that the process of creation can
begin once again.

To Emerson it was vital to figure this contrast even more dramatically. For him also the centripetal stroke of the mind was a
movement to knowledge, but it was starkly opposed to creative

expression. Creation proceeds from fullness but is conceived in emptiness. For penetrating insight or inspired creativity to occur, the mind must first divest itself entirely of its world, its attachments, itself. The inspired artist is the artist without obligations. He does not appeal to time or history; he has no past at his back.[17] Authentic worlds would arise only in a soul purged of self-interest, a soul in which all vestiges of previous creation had been systematically burned up and destroyed. In practice this was the lesson of self-reliance. The source of creation might be conceived as a resplendent sun, but in mundane experience it always lay outside the compass of the individual mind. Practically speaking, to rely on the Self meant for Emerson to empty the self—to wait in solitude and darkness, with patience and "in entire humility." Only here would the sun dawn. "To create my own world," Emerson reveals to us, what is required is "the purification of my soul." This is the basis of virtue; this is the key that "opes the palace of eternity" (CW, I, 38).

In his grand centrifugal phases, Emerson presents his revelation in proclamations of purple and gold. But these royal affirmations of the Self tend to disguise the fact that the way that leads to it is one of poverty and negation. Self-reliant optimism was really just an excited perturbation of the old Christian world-weariness. His expressions of it vary, but the method, the rule, he adopted for self-culture was the same one he absorbed from the piety and teachings of Mary Moody Emerson, his Puritan ancestors, and the Quaker friends: "do not shine," said Fox, "but lie low in the Lord's power." The way to realize the Self was to empty the self. The way to redeem the creation was to withdraw from it. Christ's *kenosis*, originally a way of conceiving the Incarnation, became in the lives of his worshippers a rule of life. For Emerson it also became a rule of nature and a rule of art. The artist's sacrifice to the source of his inspiration was modeled on the redemptive sacrifice of Christ. Here is Emerson's revelation as it is conceived in "The Poet."

> It is a secret which every intellectual man quickly learns, that, beyond the energy of his possessed and conscious intellect, he is capable of a new energy (as of an intellect dou-

bled on itself), by abandonment to the nature of things; that, beside his privacy of power as an individual man, there is a great public power, on which he can draw, by unlocking, at all risks, his human doors, and suffering the ethereal tides to roll and circulate through him: then he is caught up into the life of the Universe, his speech is thunder, his thought law, and his words are universally intelligible as the plants and animals. (CW, III, 15–16)

For the poet, as for the pietist and Quaker, newness of life proceeds by way of abandonment. To be filled with the light of vision he must make of himself an empty vessel. Humility is as much a virtue for Emerson the transcendentalist as it was for Mary Moody Emerson. It has hardly gone out of fashion or been consigned to the moldering annals of some faith gone by. On the contrary, it has risen to new precedence, since for Emerson it is no longer even just an ideal of faith—it is the law of all creation. Here the boundary between religious and artistic inspiration, always elusive in the writings of the Transcendentalists, completely disappears. Self-reliance is not simply a secular virtue, it is a religious imperative. So when in his journal Emerson writes that self-reliance is "the law and constitution of good writing," it is, significantly, a "meek" self-reliance (JMN, V, 92). For Emerson, inspired writing, like every other creative experience in life, proceeds by way of emptiness. And this in practice is what self-reliance really means.

In the wake of self-sacrifice, on a cloud of forgetting, the mind sinks back into itself. It reclines onto the ground of its own emptiness. There quietly, without the sound of angel harp or trumpet, light appears and the creation begins. But in Emerson's imaginative conception insight is still welcomed as the Bridegroom from heaven, its advent into the arms of a waiting nature depicted as the divine marriage. Once again he comes to quicken nature with his piercing glances, and once again nature yields to him a new creation. It is the Apocalypse all over again, interiorized, to be sure; attenuated, somewhat; and displaced from its biblical context to a psychology of inspiration; but it retains all its essential features. Here is the submerged apocalypse of "Intellect."

In the intellect constructive, which we popularly designate
by the word Genius, we observe the same balance of two
elements, as in intellect receptive. The constructive intellect produces thoughts, sentences, poems, plans, designs,
systems. It is the generation of the mind, the marriage of
thought with nature. To genius must always go two gifts,
the thought and the publication. The first is revelation,
always a miracle, which no frequency of occurrence, or incessant study can ever familiarize, but which must always
leave the inquirer stupid with wonder. It is the advent of
truth into the world, a form of thought now, for the first
time, bursting into the universe, a child of the old eternal
soul, a piece of genuine and immeasureable greatness.
(CW, II, 198)

With the advent of spirit, man and nature are filled by "unfail-
ing fountains." Once again the climate of paradise prevails. Man
"rests upon the bosom of God" and draws upon "inexhaustible
power" (CW, I, 38). The marriage of spirit and nature is consummated, and with the consummation comes the generation of the
new heavens and earth. This is where the apocalyptic vision of
Saint John ends—with the creation; and this is also the end of
Emerson's revelation: "Build, therefore, your own world." But
from the time of his childhood Emerson had been steeped in the
sobering assurance that the new heavens and earth would only
come on the heels of holocaust. That is why his famous exhortation "to build . . . your own world" is not the most crucial sentence
of *Nature*'s peroration. The more self-effacing sentence that follows it is: "As fast as you conform your life to the pure idea in your
mind, that will unfold its great proportions" (CW, I, 45). "Conform" should be read with all the gravity of "sacrifice," for this is
what Emerson builds into it. It is the crucial word here, bearing
much of the weight of the centuries-old cross.
This last purification of life leads directly into the naturalized
messianic vision that concludes *Nature*—the coming of the summer sun from the south. Before it the snowbanks melt and the
face of the earth turns green. The Kingdom of God is at hand. But
here the biblical revelation we have come to expect does not actu-

ally follow. The text Emerson chooses to end *Nature* does not come from the Book of Revelation. Instead he invokes his favorite passage from Luke: "the Kingdom of God cometh not with observation." There would be no cosmic fireworks, no outward show. "Behold, the Kingdom of God is within you" (Lk. 17.20–21). It was something to be seen now and not in the future, here and not in the skies above. The Kingdom is not a new world; it is just the same old world transfigured in vision. For Emerson also the apocalypse was a matter of "perfect sight." But in his formulation of Luke, he does some revising of his own. Here it is not the Kingdom of God "which cometh not with observation," but "the Kingdom of man over nature." As in Luke, it is still an apocalypse of vision, but it is not the vision of anything in particular. Emerson's Kingdom begins once man has taken nature into himself, dissolved it, made it one with Spirit. The creation which springs from *Nature*'s apocalypse is vision. The climax of *Nature*'s ascending spiral, the marriage of man and nature in "Spirit," leads no further than "Prospects." What is seen there has yet to be realized. And this is where the reader comes in.

Revision

Emerson was not interested in burdening the world with yet more creation. His vision is his creation. He arrests *Nature* at the point just before it begins to harden into a new world. Throughout *Nature* this is where the accent falls—on the vision, the prospects—which explains the well-attested preponderance here and throughout Emerson's writings of the images and metaphors of seeing.[18] The eye, we remember, is the first circle: at once the emblem of revelation and "the best of artists." By virtue of its structure and the laws of light, the eye turns mass "into a well colored and shaded globe" (CW, I, 12). The eye is the symbol for the world because it is the source and essence of the world. Emerson felt comfortable in assimilating the world to the eye, because for him vision was not only the distinctive operation of the eye, it was the nature of Reason itself. In the famous letter of 1834 to his brother Edward, Emerson explains his conception of Reason as contrasted with the Understanding: "Now that I have used the words, let me ask you do you draw the distinction of Milton Coleridge and the Germans between Reason and Understanding? I think it a philosophy itself and like all truth very practical. . . . Reason is the highest faculty of the soul—what we mean often by the soul itself; it never *reasons,* never proves, it simply perceives, it is vision" (L, I, 412–13). In *Nature,* Emerson extended the power of Reason even further: "When the eye of Reason opens, to outline and surface are at once added, grace and expression. These proceed from imagination and affection, and abate somewhat of the angular distinctness of objects. If the Reason be stimulated to more earnest vision, outlines and surfaces become transparent, and are no longer seen; causes and spirits are seen through them" (CW, I, 30). For his views of Reason, Emerson still chiefly follows Coleridge. Reason did not operate by ways and means, or by process of calculation. Reason was immediate. It knew because it saw. Like vision, Reason was union with the things known, unmediated cognition.[19] It was only in the nature of things, therefore, to figure Reason as the eye of the world.

Emerson owes an incalculable debt to Coleridge for his views of human reason, but he does not follow him into his tangle of distinctions regarding its subsidiary faculties and powers. This is particularly evident in the case of the imagination. He accepts the basic Coleridgean distinction between fancy and the imagination, but he does not bother to refine his conception of imagination any further than Reason itself. The highest activity of the Imagination is still the same as that of Reason proper—vision. "The Fancy takes the world as it stands and selects pleasing groups by apparent relations. The Imagination is Vision, regards the world as symbolical and pierces the emblem for the real sense, sees all external objects as types" (JMN, V, 76).

Emerson was not the scholastic hairsplitter Coleridge was, but there is a deeper reason why he tended characteristically to limit the artist's highest faculty to seeing. He knew at firsthand the technical requirements imposed by an artist's craft, and practiced them scrupulously; but for him it was the vision and not the *poesis* that defined the highest elevation of the artistic vocation. At these rarefied heights, the vision of artist and mystic seer was the same.

> In the highest moments, we are vision. There is nothing that can be called gratitude nor properly joy. The soul is raised over passion. It seeth nothing so much as Identity. It is a Perceiving that Truth and Right ARE. Hence it becomes a perfect Peace out of the knowing that all things will go well. Vast spaces of Nature—the Atlantic ocean, the South Sea; vast intervals of time—years, centuries, are annihilated to it. (JMN, V, 467)

In the instant of revelation, vision and being coalesce. The next instant inaugurates the new heaven and earth. By disposition, Emerson chose not to follow his vision into its new creation. He preferred to balance himself at the brink of the apocalypse, before the fixing of nature, in a vision of all possibilities. He mastered his precipitous position by learning to retire inwardly even as he pitched forward into creative expression. The effect, ironically, was to keep his vision burning at an apocalyptic heat.

The epitome of Emerson's distinctive apocalyptic vision is found in the notorious "transparent eyeball" passage of *Nature*. Unfortunately, criticism has never completely recovered from Christopher Cranch's funny lampoon of Emerson as a spindly-legged figure with a gigantic balloon-shaped eyeball for a head. In what is otherwise an appreciative treatment of Emerson, Jonathan Bishop gives the eyeball passage its coup de grace: "the speaker, the I, is innocently absurd at best; the rhythm is a coarse parody of the watchful casualness of the other sentence; and the language is vapid."[20] My own tendency is usually to lay the vehemence of such reactions to a lack of imagination or versatility on the part of the reader, but in any case, Bishop's criticism, though understandable, is one of taste not substance. Emerson wrote to be admired, but not just to be admired. And this famous passage is one case where the function of hierophant takes precedence over the function of poet. Not only the context of this epiphany, but also its structure and the rhythm and sound of the language

itself, are conceived in accordance with the double movement of
the interior apocalypse that he envisioned. Much of what I have
written in these chapters finds exemplification and minute verification in this gawky but oracular text. It is a crucial passage for
any investigation into the religious implications of Emerson's
prose, but surprisingly enough, few have bothered to analyze it in
the detail it deserves.

The epiphany as a whole presents itself in two parts or stages.
The first, beginning with "crossing" and ending with gladness
and fear, paves the way for the revelation; while the second, beginning with "standing" and ending properly with "God," enacts it.
Both of these sections stand out from the paragraph in which they
are embedded by their sudden introduction of the first person.
They are interrupted by a brief return to nature, "in the woods
too," and the third person.

Not all of the passage is as artless as the section in which the
eyeball appears. Even for Jonathan Bishop the first part frames
one of Emerson's most auspicious sentences, just as the second
part contains his most uncouth. Part of the beauty of this famous
sentence comes from its highly suggestive character: "Crossing a
bare common, in snow puddles, at twilight, under a clouded sky,
without having in my thoughts any occurrence of special good
fortune, I have enjoyed a perfect exhilaration. Almost I fear to
think how glad I am." In sharp contrast to the second section,
there is much in this first sentence of the epiphany with which we
still feel at home. We are presented with a real world—"a bare
common, in snow puddles, at twilight, under a clouded sky"—not
some grotesque abstraction. What we, along with Jonathan Bishop, appreciate about the first sentence is its cultivated, unruffled
tone and its familiar atmosphere. We too have had our moments
of exhilaration, though perhaps not quite ecstasy; and we too
have soaked our shoes on a New England or other such common,
in the puddles of a February thaw. In fact, Emerson himself
seems to work his sentence up from some such actual experience,
as the Journal entries which he drew on for his formulation indicate (JMN, IV, 355; JMN, V, 24–25). We begin our crossing, in
short, where we must—in the familiar. This is our common
ground: snow puddles, twilight, and clouded sky. If, for the sake of

experiment, we were to subject this sentence to the old fourfold mode of exegesis which biblical commentators once practiced on the Bible, this resolution of the sentence into particular times and places would be fully accommodated within the literal mode. But the sentence itself begins to strain at the literal frame of reference when it admits foreign elements into its world of easy familiarity. The urbane "I have enjoyed a perfect exhilaration" is followed by the discordant "Almost I fear to think how glad I am." A stroll along the common does not justify this disconcerting coda, with its uncanny mixture of gladness and fear. Something more is going on here, something strange, perhaps awful, which the narrator is just beginning to realize and dread. Unexpectedly, a vertical axis has intersected at the horizontal. In 1849 Emerson decided to draw the angle thus generated to sharper tension still: "Almost I fear to think how glad I am" became "I am glad to the brink of fear," making it even clearer that after the crossing we readers ought to begin reading vertically as well as horizontally.

The first thing such a reading suggests to us is that Emerson's common ground may indeed have an allegorical as well as a literal reference. Like Bunyan's City of Destruction it is our common point of departure. The "bare common" we cross itself constitutes an intersection or crossing: it is a place where town and forest intermingle. But as the triple volley of locatives that follow suggests, this common is more than a coincidence of topographies. Here winter anticipates spring "in snow puddles," day shades off into night "at twilight," and heaven descends to earth "under a clouded sky." Emerson selects for the site of his revelation a place on the borders of time and space. This is appropriate, for as Victor Turner points out, the site of the hierophany is always liminal. Here, betwixt and between, is the place where the sacred and profane cross over.[21]

At first blush there is not much in the site of this revelation that extends beyond the perimeter of Concord Common. But a closer look will suggest that Emerson's images have wider reference than that. In the first chapter, I noted the curious domination of winter in the seasonal representation of *Nature*. There is textual evidence that for Emerson the barren whiteness of the snow was imaginatively associated with the apocalyptic imagery of the Bible. Here, once again, winter upstages summer, and it does so at just the point when it gives way to spring. But for Emerson there is a related image which bears an even greater apocalyptic significance than the snow, and that is the cloud that conveys it. Here in *Nature* a "clouded sky" is the last thing we see before we are caught up in "exhilaration." And throughout the Journals and notebooks, cloud imagery is frequently associated with apocalypse or moments of epiphany. When Emerson describes the afternoon of transport he spent at Mount Auburn in the spring of 1834, he is sure to include his observation of "the clouds that hang their significant drapery over us" (JMN, IV, 273). In 1832, as we have seen, "a cloudy lonely walk" is cited as possible circumstances for a breakthrough by "the divine inmate," who himself speaks to us "out of clouds and darkness" (JMN, IV, 28). Emerson uses this last phrase as early as 1823 in an entry that draws explicitly on the apocalyptic writings of the Bible. Here again "cloud and darkness" are the veils with which the "Lord of the Universe" clothes himself (JMN, II, 126). And as we have seen, "Gnothi Seauton," that crowning expression of Emerson's later revelation of the God within, upholds this old way of seeing—here also the veil consists of cloud (JMN, III, 290). In one of the journal entries that Emerson drew on in his construction of the "eyeball" passage, he approves Charles Bell's view that "no hour, no state of the atmosphere but corresponded to some state of the mind" (JMN, IV, 355), and it seems clear from such instances as the above that for Emerson clouds were the precursors or accompaniments of revelation.

His license for this is clearly biblical. Throughout the Bible, Old Testament and New, the Messiah comes to earth on clouds of glory. Here, for instance, is the way Saint Mark describes it: "But in those days, after that tribulation, the sun shall be darkened, and the moon shall not give its light. And the stars of heaven shall fall, and the powers that are in the heavens shall be shaken. And then shall they see the Son of man coming in the clouds, with great power and glory" (Mk. 13.24–26). Saint John's "Revelation" also has the Son of man seated on a cloud (Rev. 14.14–15). Here and in other such figurative texts, by a process of imaginative sympathy, the cloud image begins to coalesce with other images of the divine manifestation, including those of white raiment, snow, or transparency. Emerson feels all these biblical associations, and it is probable that many of his early readers did also.[22] Behind Emerson's passage over snow puddles, in twilight, under a clouded sky is the apocalyptic paradigm: from the blankness of annihilation to the descent of the Son of man on clouds of glory. Indeed, it is an epiphany which disguises epithalamion, since here at the common crossing is where the marriage of the heavens and the earth, of spirit and nature, really takes place.

But if Emerson places his epiphany in a biblical cosmos, it is at a considerable distance from the Revelation of Saint John. The biblical myth exists here only in the intertextual nimbus that surrounds these images. In the light of common sense, nothing can be seen here that has not been thoroughly naturalized and assimilated to everyday experience: Saint John's remote and inaccessible island mount gives way to a level common; his vision, esoteric and rarefied, has become a possibility for the common man; dazzling eschaton is replaced by a democratic present.

Emerson minimizes the allegorical and mythical senses of his sentence in order to highlight the universal moral and spiritual sense. What he means to emphasize here is the bounty of the divine nature. Revelation is not confined to some remote time or place, or specific attitudes or works; it is free and universally available. "The Kingdom of God," these lines confirm, "is within you."

Unlike the first stage of the revelation, which moves along various horizontal and vertical axes of crossing, the revelation proper is spherical and circular. It originates not in a movement of crossing but from a standing center which in the vision that follows becomes the birthplace of a new world. From this still center the revelation expands violently on all sides. Also in contrast with the first stage is the fact that here in the heart of the revelation nothing of the familiar and everyday remains. Everything is formed on abstraction. Emerson filters every concreteness from his formulation, with the one notable exception of the giant eyeball. As various commentators have noted, the eyeball

image may have its source in Plotinus or other mystical philosophers.[23] But this does not explain why Emerson decided to thrust
such an artless and grotesque image into what until that passage
is a smooth and well-modulated prose. While this sudden loosening of stylistic constraints may constitute a lapse of decorum, it
does not constitute a lapse of religious authenticity. The supernatural always breaks in this way, as the stories of Flannery
O'Connor, for example, are designed to show. At the onset of
revelation there is nothing decorous in the divine. It shatters
through habitual consciousness with brute force. It appears not as
we would expect, but as we would least expect—strange, often
shocking, wholly other. Fear and trembling, not contentment, are
the emotions it arouses. *Nature*'s famous epiphany deliberately
dispenses with the style of a Victorian gentleman in order to
admit the sharp hieratic utterings of the oracle. Here Emerson's
smooth sentences break and splinter to give way to the rough
beast, the intrusive and unsettling apocalypse.

While the oracular centerpiece of *Nature*'s revelation may lack
the suggestiveness and grace of the preliminary passage of crossing, it is not devoid of poetic devices. Indeed, scansion of these
lines will reveal that they are carefully designed and deployed to
approximate and to recapitulate the double movement of revelation I have tried to identify throughout *Nature*. Though it may
seem unorthodox to analyze this section of prose with the attention ordinarily reserved for poetry, it takes such reading to see
how completely the impulses of Emerson's pen are guided by the
movements of revelation. The structure of his oracle is easiest to
see when it is set out in verse form:

> Standing on the bare ground,—
> my head bathed by the blithe air,
> and uplifted into infinite space,—
> all mean egotism vanishes.
> I become a transparent eye-ball.
> I am nothing.
> I see all.
> The currents of the Universal Being circulate through me;
> I am part or particle of God.

What results from such representation, as even a cursory look will
show, is a configuration whose right margin roughly follows the
outline of a left-facing parabola or the side of an hourglass. The
edge defined by the ends of the lines at the top of the stanza con-
tracts at the center of the revelation—"I am nothing. I see all"—
and then stretches out again as the vision unfolds. This structure
merely conforms to the sense of the vision, which also describes a
movement between expansion and contraction. We begin, to all
appearances, "standing on the bare ground." However, this is no
longer the "bare common" of the previous passage—some particular place among many—it is rather "*the* bare ground." This is a
definite ground: we might even say, the world's exclusive ground.
It is not a ground in the world but the ground of the world. The
reason we are treated entirely to abstraction here, why we see
nothing of clouds and snow puddles, is that from now on our standpoint is spirit. In this way the first three lines introduce the great
sphere of being, the globe of vision, and by implication contrast
with the phenomenal setting of vision on "a bare common." This is
one sense of the revision suggested here by "the bare ground." A
second is that by virtue of it Emerson can emphasize the necessary
basis of his vision in emptiness. "The bare ground" purges the
original setting of all particularity and fixes the source of vision in
the singularity suggested by the spondee. The second line recurs
and responds to the fixed establishment of "the bare ground" with
"blithe air," its own final spondee. Only at this point in the emer-
gence of vision, the singularity is already loosening: the line begins
to unfold itself accentually and syllabically as the vision expands
upwardly. Already in the second line the bare ground of the vision
is becoming insphered and dilated. Phonically, this process of expansion is encouraged by the internal rhyme of "air" with "bare,"
and especially by the repetition of the alliterative and aspirated
b's. The rhythmic alliteration and internal rhyme lighten the
heavy assertion of the first line and produce an almost incantatory
effect which helps to convey the swirling upward movement of the
revelation. In the third line the heavy *b*'s and *g*'s give way to the
volatile *f*'s and *i*'s of "uplifted" and "infinite," while "ground" and
"air" extend up into "space."

Through the alliterative incantation of these three lines, we are

lifted into a state of expanded fullness. The I stretches way outside its usual boundaries and makes of itself a new world. And
here begins the quick succession of spiritual pulsations which is
distinctive of Emerson's revelation. With the sudden advent of
this new power of Self, the old self instantly evaporates—"all
mean egotism vanishes." The rhythm and metrical arrangement
of this line persuasively enact the destructive stroke of the apocalypse. The heavy cadences of the phrase "all mean egotism" and
the clenched and muscular tautness of the word "egotism" itself
are effortlessly loosened and neutralized by the short open syllables of "vanishes." Our awareness here is withdrawn from cosmic
fullness to personal emptiness. The personal self is sacrificed, the
creation is dissolved. In contrast to the last syllables of the preceding three lines, the last syllable of "vanishes" is unaccented.
There is no sense of fullness here, only emptiness and vacuity.
But no sooner than the self becomes aware of its own emptiness, a
new and more robust self is born: "I become a transparent eyeball." New self generates itself in the form of a globe, a giant
eyeball, which rises out of the ashes of a vanished ego. Once again
the movement of revelation repeats itself. The seer realizes his
fullness in order to sacrifice it. He recurs again to the source of his
being and again realizes, "I am nothing"; the response—"I see
all." From fullness of being, the seer pulsates instantaneously
back to emptiness out to fullness back to emptiness and out to
fullness.

   Each of these last three lines, "I become a transparent eyeball,"
"I am nothing," and "I see all," represents an autonomous realization, but they are connected by a movement from "become" to
"am" to "see." In this context also, the double movement of revelation may be seen in terms of the centrifugal and centripetal forces
of the spirit. The actions of becoming and seeing are centrifugal;
they create meaning, form, relationship. But their momentum
depends on a recurrent movement of being, a retiring from previous creation and the recognition of Self stripped of all conditions.
The apex of Emerson's vision is gnosis: "I see all." It is a vision so
pure that it has not yet descended out of the crown of being. It is
the same vision that Blake cultivated—when "every thing would
appear to man as it is, infinite." Emerson aspires also to remain

at this apocalyptic crest, but it was not his experience. From this vision of pure being, the revelation falls out into ancillary cognitions of relation and emotions of love and beauty. "The currents of the Universal Being circulate through me; I am part or particle of God." The revelation proper is losing its force when the seer has regained the presence of mind to say: "The name of the nearest friend sounds then foreign and accidental. To be brothers, to be acquaintances,—master or servant, is then a trifle and a disturbance. I am the lover of uncontained and immortal beauty."

Plotinus and the mystical philosophers of Europe were not the only sources for Emerson's conception of the eye as an emblem of being. His own bout with temporary blindness in 1825 had convinced him of the indissoluble connection between vision and spiritual health. Emerson prized his "musical eyes" above all the senses. Yet earlier than any of these influences was the Bible. Here also the eye is the window of the soul (Lk. 11.34), and vision the key to salvation. When he gave his address to the students at Waterville College in 1841, Emerson leaned heavily on the text of Proverbs 29.18: "where there is no vision, the people perish." And, as we have seen, his treatment of transparency in *Nature* and throughout his writings owes much to the images and paradigm of biblical apocalypse. Indeed, if Emerson's imaginative reliance on the Book of Revelation teaches us anything, it is that for him revelation was itself essentially vision.

This is why, in spite of Emerson's sometime claims to the contrary, nature could never supply the model for *Nature*. The book is not a transcript of nature except insofar as you presume nature to be a transcript of something else. *Nature* does not describe a thing, but a movement. It enacts a series of transformations in the relationship between nature and spirit. And these transformations articulate themselves at every level through the double movement of revelation. Each stroke of expansion creates a new vision; each stroke of renunciation and contraction abolishes that vision to make way for the new. This is the essence of Emerson's revelation. It is not vision, but revision. Left to itself, he knew, vision—any vision—quickly grew old and out of date. True revelation does not age, because it refers endlessly to itself. It is a circuit of self-referral. This is why Emerson refuses simply to represent any particular view or views and leave it at that. What he wants to represent is how views are come to—and then superseded. It is not truth he respects, but truthing, as it were—what Thoreau called improving the nick of time.

But this is where the Bible comes back into the picture. No meaningful vision occurs in an experiential or contextual darkness, even a vision like *Nature*'s, which is revision. Without connection and contrast to a present or previous state of experience, it will have no force to transform. A vision without reference to its previous forms only makes of itself another prison, however large or palatial. Meaningful vision depends upon prevision. *Nature*'s revision, like any vision, turns in a consciousness of its predecessors. And for Emerson this indispensable prevision is clearly the Christian Bible.

The spin-off of this point, as I have suggested throughout these chapters, itself constitutes a revision which, in effect, throws into question the whole tradition of criticism which insists on seeing some "organic principle" at work in transcendentalist writing.[24] Whatever it is that is defined as "organic" in *Nature,* and it is hard to know precisely what that would mean, it does not arise in terms of nature but in contrast to, or revision of, previous such texts, the Bible above all. Properly generalized, the intertextuality of *Nature* issues from the nature of revelation itself. At its conservative pole language means to represent; at its creative pole it changes. *Nature* is language at its most unsettling. It is not essentially a rhetoric of representation but a rhetoric of provocation. It is designed to move the reader, to take him or her through the transformations that constitute its overall significance. *Nature* offers its own representations, of course, but in the end it is all feigning. It does so because of the requirements of experience—of vision and of language. For all speakers, but especially for the rhetorician, words move on the basis of their previous meanings. All speech is indebted. "It is years and nations that guide my pen," quipped Emerson (JMN, IV, 27).

In *Nature* Emerson set out to offer his contemporaries a new revelation, but he was shrewd enough to know that revelation would never be new unless it made implicit reference to what it meant before. In most respects, the relationship between the old and new revelations was one of tension, if not antagonism. *Nature* implies the biblical revelation in order to distinguish and distance itself from it. The Bible is overthrown to make way for new possibilities. But then, if my analysis of Emerson's revelation is accurate, this is very much in the nature of the book.[25]

Such textual hostility alone is revealing here, but there is reason to think the relationship may be even more intimate than that. Emerson relied upon the old revelation to produce the new, because he knew that such reliance was central to the movement of revision. But he also knew that the Bible itself constituted a record of such revision. Emerson's favorite passage from Luke, the one with which he ends *Nature,* is of course the prime example of a messianic revision. He embraced this particular vision of the Kingdom within, but more important to him perhaps was the impulse that led to it. The relationship between type and antitype, Old Testament and New, literal and spiritual sense, by means of which the Christian Bible came to define itself, grew out of the same revisionary tension that animated his own book. In the understanding of his readers, the Bible at best served Emerson as a pretext, but rightly read, it was a pretext that itself incorporated the whole structure of revelation.

4 The Rhetoric of Revelation

The best part of Emersonianism is, it breeds the giant that destroys itself. Who wants to be any man's mere follower? lurks behind every page. No teacher ever taught, that has so provided for his pupil's setting up independently—no truer evolutionist.
—Whitman

Whoever is a teacher through and through takes all things seriously only in relation to his students—even himself.
—Nietzsche

The circle of *Nature*'s readers has always been a more or less restricted one, though by no means a very homogeneous one. It is true that Emerson was pleasantly surprised to hear that within a month of its first appearance five hundred copies had already been sold. This was, he thought, "a good deliverance" for a book "purely literary or philosophical" (L, II, 42). Yet, despite this spring tide of interest, the sales of *Nature* soon diminished to a mere trickle: it took another eight years before the remainder of the initial run of fifteen hundred copies was completely sold out.[1]

To be sure, *Nature* has never enjoyed the vogue of a best-seller; its appeal has been more limited than that, and its life, proportionally, a good deal longer. It is a demanding book. It belongs to that class of literature which Thoreau said you had to stand on tiptoe to read. Up there what you read depends on how much you see, which in turn depends on what kind of person you are. At this elevation the reader helps write the book. Perhaps this goes some way to explain why in the whole history of American literature *Nature* still appears as such an anomaly. It is hard to classify because it is hard to identify. And it is hard to identify because, perhaps, no two readers wind up seeing exactly the same book. Is it a sermon, a poem, a philosophical tract, or something else? In the final analysis, this depends on how you complete it, since, sentences on the page, it is one of the most inchoate books there is.

This incompleteness or suggestiveness may also explain the sharp divergence of response among those readers who do make their way over the precipitous canyons and outcroppings of *Nature*'s texture. A short survey will tend to show that now as before readers' responses are apt to cluster around the extremes of exhilaration, on the one hand, and exasperation on the other—neutral and lukewarm readers having been comparatively rare. To read Emerson is to strive with him: in the end you either throw him down or privilege him on your shelf. No one reads *Nature* understandingly without considerable personal investment. And even among those readers who see in it doctrines pernicious and disruptive, there has been a consciousness of the special responsibility charged by Emerson's sentences. Few commentators, pro or con, have been as precise in describing this experience of reading *Nature,* as well as its possible pitfalls, as Francis Bowen, whose 1837 critique was one of the first to draw the battle lines between the orthodox Unitarians and this alien "New School."

> We find beautiful writing and sound philosophy in this little work; but the effect is injured by occasional vagueness of expression, and by a vein of mysticism, that per-

vades the writer's whole course of thought. The highest
praise that can be accorded to it, is, that it is a *suggestive*
book, for no one can read it without tasking his faculties to
the utmost, and relapsing into fits of severe meditation.
But the effort of perusal is often painful, the thoughts excited are frequently bewildering, and the results to which
they lead us, uncertain and obscure. The reader feels as in
a disturbed dream, in which shows of surpassing beauty
are around him, and he is conversant with disembodied
spirits, yet all the time he is harassed by an uneasy sort of
consciousness, that the whole combination of phenomena is
fantastic and unreal.[2]

Though on the surface the last two sentences of this paragraph
seem intentionally less flattering than the first two, it is probably
not the case that Emerson would have found them any less pleasing. It is interesting how the mood they set up presages the one in
which we find ourselves in "Experience." Here, similarly, "sleep
lingers . . . about our eyes" while "ghost-like we glide through nature" (CW, III, 27). That in reading *Nature* the reader should find
himself transported as if "in a disturbed dream" may not have been
what Emerson specifically intended in 1836, but he certainly
seems to have sanctioned such possibilities by 1844. Indeed, even
by the time of the composition of "Circles" several years before he
finished "Experience," he was going out of his way to warn his
readers about the dangers of security: "People wish to be settled:
only as far as they are unsettled, is there any hope for them" (CW,
II, 189). The fact that the "uneasy sort of consciousness" Bowen
experienced upon reading *Nature* was characterized by "disembodied spirits" and "fantastic and unreal" phenomena was not, in
the final analysis, really material. It was crucial, however, that the
writing avoided the very real danger of saddling the reader with
some dead weight of certainty. The purpose of *Nature,* as I have
tried to indicate, was not to stop the creation but to get it going
again. To find that his book had proved so "suggestive" must have
been for Emerson "highest praise" indeed.

An Easterly Reading

In the summer during which Emerson was giving the finishing touches to his book, he announced in his Journal what had always been and would always continue to be for him the highest function of literature. And here, not surprisingly, the model he looked to was Revelation and even the literal Word of God. "It is the property of the divine to be reproductive. The harvest is seed. The good sermon becomes a text in the hearer's mind. That is the good book which sets us at work. The highest science is prophecy. Jesus is but the harbinger and announcer of the Comforter to come, and his continual office is to make himself less to us by making us demand more" (JMN, V, 180–81). To the centuries-long debate about the true and proper function of literature, Emerson contributes a startling new voice. The oldest answer—*mimesis*—was Aristotle's; this one Emerson publicly embraces but practially eschews.[3] Other answers, such as to delight or to instruct, also venerable, he all but ignores. For Emerson, the best, the most consequential, literature does not imitate, instruct, or delight—it galvanizes. Provocation, not edification, is its concern. But by this he did not mean that the poet should be a rabble-rouser; baiting the reader for its own sake was not the point. What he meant was to provoke in the root sense of calling forth—to stimulate in others what was productive in oneself. Indeed, for Emerson, to provoke meant to procreate. The most universal writer does not mobilize language in the service of leisure or the authorized particulars of science, ethics, or even the eternal verities. He works at the root of life; he vivifies and unstops the movements of mind. He is not concerned with the organs and structure of the fully formed result but with the energy that conceives them. "Books," Emerson insisted in his address "The American Scholar," "are for nothing but to inspire" (CW, I, 56), and a year later, in an even more famously iconoclastic delivery, he rejected the significance of all communications but the most vital: "Truly speaking, it is not instruction, but provocation, that I can receive from another soul" (CW, I, 80). Emerson's poetics may seem primitive, but for him this ensures their proximity to truth. In the will and designs of a masterful teacher, such provocation conditions the ground of revelation. And that in the end is all that really matters. "A wise writer will feel that the ends of study and composition are best answered by announcing undiscovered regions of thought, and so communicating, through hope, new activity to the torpid spirit" (CW, I, 41). Here, in the context significantly of "Prospects," is Emerson's strategy as he suggests it in *Nature*. He deals in power, not the finished product. The final creation is as much the responsibility of the reader, and it exists, as yet, only on the level of vision and prophecy. *Nature* is only a virtual text; it takes the revelations of the reader to give it fiber and sap.

This participation of the reader in the unfolding of *Nature* is what Bowen alluded to in 1837: "it is a *suggestive* book, for no one can read it without tasking his faculties to the utmost, and relapsing into fits of severe meditation." What he epitomizes for us here is the experience to which countless persevering readers, past and present, have been prompted in their perusal of *Nature*. This is not his experience only; it is the experience of any reader who makes a sincere effort to come to terms with what *Nature* means. Emerson does not convey this experience exactly, he precipitates it. His fascinating sentences lead us on and then regularly throw us back on ourselves. And this, of course, is where the real reading occurs, for the self, as always in Emerson's prose, is the primary text. This self-referral is the fruit and purpose of all right reading. And if our own experience of reading *Nature* leaves us in any doubt, Emerson makes his point explicitly elsewhere.

> Undoubtedly there is a right way of reading,—so it be sternly subordinated. Man Thinking must not be subdued by his instruments. Books are for the scholar's idle times. When he can read God directly, the hour is too precious to be wasted in other men's transcripts of their readings. But when the intervals of darkness come, as come they must,— when the soul seeth not, when the sun is hid, and the stars withdraw their shining—we repair to the lamps which were kindled by their ray to guide our steps to the East again, where the dawn is. We hear that we may speak. The Arabian proverb says, "A fig tree looking on a fig tree, becometh fruitful." (CW, I, 57)

If books are for the scholar's idle times, this, of course, includes
Emerson's own book also. But so long as we are at it, so long as
the sun and stars have "withdrawn their shining," we ought to
approach our reading in the proper light. Though the full glory of
the Self may have yet to dawn on us, we still have its surrogate
lamps to help us keep our orientation. In this reformulation of
Emerson's important figure of easting, he provides us with the
suggestion that the "rule" of inspiration he wondered about in
1835 should also be applied to the mundane process of reading
itself. Whether nature is the object of our contemplation, or some
other mortal's book, the mechanics must be the same.

As my citation of Bowen's reading experience has been intended to suggest, something like this easterly reading is exactly
the response Emerson's rhetoric actually elicits in us. *Nature*'s
design is on us, since, in the final analysis, it is the reader who is
the "end" of nature. The rest of this chapter sheds light on this
ulterior design and provides the fuller commentary to this key
passage cited also previously, which, woven into the fabric of the
text, provides the author's prescription for reading—no matter
what the level.

> . . . the best read naturalist who lends an entire and devout
> attention to truth, will see that there remains much to
> learn of his relation to the world, and that it is not to be
> learned by any addition or subtraction or other comparison
> of known quantities, but is arrived at by untaught sallies of
> the spirit, by a continual self-recovery, and by entire humil-
> ity. (CW, I, 39)

"The Voice of Many Waters"

Emerson's literary reputation might be less equivocal than it is
were it not for the sporadic complaints of disjointedness, redundancy, or inconsistency with which his writing has sometimes
been greeted. His famously biting remark on the topic of consis-

tency indicates that he was aware of the possible grounds for such criticism (CW, II, 33). And in spite of such official declarations of nonconformity to accepted standards of expository decorum, in moments of despondency or pique he himself sometimes voiced misgivings. In one such fit Emerson described his writing habits to Carlyle this way: "Here I sit and read and write with very little system and as far as regards composition with the most fragmentary result: paragraphs incompressible each sentence an infinitely repellent particle" (CEC, 185). In fact, the grainy and disjointed texture of Emerson's prose might suggest to some that the discursive faculty is one human use that *Nature* is hardly competent to serve.

This is of course not the response that we would anticipate from a first glance over *Nature*'s neatly arranged headings and subheadings. The reaction first enjoined on us is one evoked by rational discourse: eight chapters, arranged sequentially according to one overarching scheme, with an "Introduction" that formulates the initiating question and a final chapter that provides its resolution. A closer look shows that the ordering principle underlying this sequential arrangement is the ascending scale from nature's lower to its higher "uses." Each chapter itself, but explicitly "Beauty," "Language," "Discipline," and "Idealism," further subdivides the use in question according to its application to various aspects of the human personality: senses, body, intellect, conscience, reason.

This specific configuration is original, but *Nature*'s dispositional method of treatment owes much to two rhetorical models with which both Emerson and his early readers were thoroughly familiar.[4] The first was the form of the philosophic or scientific treatise, examples of which Emerson had been dipping into for years but especially in preparation for his lecture series on natural science in 1833–34. The introductory lecture for that series, "The Uses of Natural History," enumerates five advantages derived from the study of natural science that clearly anticipate, in both presentation and content, the uses catalogued in *Nature* three years later (EL, I, 5–26). Notes on Emerson's visit to the Jardin des Plantes in 1833 suggest his fascination with such scientific systems of classification and their potential applicability to the moral and spiritual life (JMN, IV, 198–200).[5] As we noted early on, following the swelling rhetoric of the exordium, *Nature*'s persona shifts suddenly into a rhetoric of philosophic demonstration, and this classificatory arrangement seems to be its structural counterpart:

> Philosophically considered, the universe is composed of Nature and the Soul. Strictly speaking, therefore, all that is separate from us, all which Philosophy distinguishes as the Not Me, that is, both nature and art, all other men and my own body, must be ranked under this name, Nature. In enumerating the values of nature and casting up their sum, I shall use the word in both senses;—in its common and in its philosophical import. (CW, I, 8).

The fact that this definitional section leaves off abruptly with the introduction of a paean to solitude in chapter 1 suggests how tentatively this philosophic rhetoric and its scientific armature ought to be taken. The sequence is not arbitrary, as we have seen with reference to the spiral that informs it, but it is difficult to see how the scholastic framework as such could be construed as anything more than a temporary convenience. As a scaffolding it served Emerson indifferently, and it was the only time in his published writing that he was to make use of it. What it does do is to set up a certain range of expectations in his readership. This was after all not a novel rhetorical form—New England readers had been used for almost a century to this kind of philosophic presentation. Indeed, there was nothing in the book's outward mode of presentation or ostensible subject that would have caused any great sensation. Its apparently academic presentation helped signal the advance perception that the truths about to be unfolded would be done so rationally and, it was hoped, instructively. This is not exactly the way things turn out, as we shall see, but it gives the right start. By virtue of what is in part a rhetorical ploy, the author serves notice to his readers that the exposition to be offered is open to—indeed requires—careful examination.

Behind the model of the learned treatise or address lay a second model for *Nature*'s architecture, more familiar to Emerson's early readers if less obvious to some of us, and that was of course the sermon. It is not necessary to consult the books and journals of early nineteenth-century Boston for the kind of dispositional rhetoric we find in *Nature,* when we can locate an even more proximate basis in the sermons preached from the Unitarian and Congregational pulpits each Sunday. The sermons of old New England, like their later successors, were calculated to ignite the faith, but from an early time also to engage and satisfy the reason. By the start of the nineteenth century, New England's ministers no longer adhered strictly to the rhetorical framework of the seventeenth-century sermon with its fourfold division of biblical text, context, doctrines, and uses, but they had by no means relaxed their emphasis on rational demonstration and argumentative proof.[6] New Englanders still looked to a learned ministry for religious guidance, and the faith these ministers cultivated was still a reasoned one. Emerson was of course a direct heir to this homiletic tradition—he was conditioned and trained in it—and this is apparent from the structure of his own sermons, which, though freer in their form than those of his forebears, regularly treat his reflections on a given biblical text in a systematic numerical order. This is as true of a late sermon such as "The Miracle of Our Being," first delivered in 1834, as it is of his earliest extant sermon, "Pray Without Ceasing," first delivered in 1826 (YES, 1–12, 203–12).

What the dispositional rhetoric of homiletic demonstration and learned disquisition have in common is an appeal to, among other things, the discursive understanding. This is the kind of appeal that Anglo-American readers would naturally come to expect of a treatise on "nature." By recurring to this familiar rhetorical form, *Nature*'s author makes an implicit claim for its logical coherence and thereby engages the reader from the start in a heightened state of critical expectation. Such critical alertness, at the very least, seems necessary if one is to accomplish the steep scaling occasioned further along in the body of the book. But here again we find evidence of a rhetorical ploy, insofar as what follows lends itself hardly at all to the processing of an ordinary discursive reading.

If our attention to the spiral design of Emerson's book suggests anything, it is that here the ostensible logical development is something of an illusion. The "progressive method," we may remember, is not "progressive" in the ordinary sense at all. Progressive for Emerson simply meant self-reflexive. And as critics from Buell to Ellison have pointed out, one characteristic feature of Emerson's prose is its ability to give the illusion of forward momentum while all along it is really coursing back on itself. Despite its scholastic paraphernalia of chapters, topic sentences, and numbered headings, *Nature* is not, in fact, an argument built upon steps and corollaries; it is variations on a theme. The governing figure of logical exposition is the line; in Emerson, as we have seen, it is the circle. From a linear treatment we expect sequence, logical progression, justification, and conclusion; and we evaluate its merit thereby. *Nature,* and the essays generally, confound such expectations. It is not fundamentally a logical demonstration; indeed, as Ellison suggests, its links and transitions are more often specious than not. *Nature* describes a circling, and as such its characteristic rhetorical move is not sequence but repetition. Often a sentence does not so much develop its precursor as paraphrase it. And the paragraph as a whole turns out to be a mere catalogue or series of restatements and substitutions, the independent constituents arranged in a kind of "discontinuous adjacency" to each other.[7] This is a rhetoric not of philosophical demonstration but of repetition, re-creation, and substitution:[8]

> To the attentive eye, each moment of the year has its own beauty, and in the same field, it beholds, every hour, a picture which was never seen before, and which shall never be seen again. The heavens change every moment, and reflect their glory or gloom on the plains beneath. The state of the crop in the surrounding farms alters the expression of the earth from week to week. The succession of native plants in the pastures and road-sides, which make the silent clock by which time tells the summer hours, will make even the divisions of the day sensible to a keen observer. The tribes of birds and insects, like the plants punctual to their time, follow each other, and the year has room for all. (CW, I, 14)

This passage from "Beauty" epitomizes the substitutive style that articulates much of the book as a whole. Here the ostensible subject is natural time, which the narrator characterizes not as continuous duration but as periodic succession; and he provides us with a series of illustrations from a revolving New England landscape. As framed, the sequence begins with a general formulation and proceeds with four successive instances rhythmically presented with the introduction of the definite article. There are no conjunctions and no specifiable logic articulating these four instances as we move from the heavens, to the condition of the crop, to the plants, to the birds and insects; they are arranged in a loosely paratactic order similarly to the passage cited previously from "Discipline." Even internally, the sense, grammar, and punctuation of these sentences manage to avoid any buildup of hypotactic configurations of meaning. The introduction of parenthetical elements such as "every hour," set off by commas; the restriction of connectives to conjunctions such as "and" or "or"; and the emphasis both in phrasing and usage on periodicity, such as "from week to week," "succession," "clock," "divisions," "punctual"—all work together to accentuate the principle of uniform and regular succession that is being illustrated.

The fiction set up here, as in the book generally, is that it is the landscape itself which suggests to us this principle of succession, when, in fact, all these moments of presentation are predicated on the projective experience of "the attentive eye." Whether nature actually changes in such a fitful fashion, we may never know; all we do know is that this is how we see it. Nature appears to the eye, to the subject, only in the shape of the present moment, and this is as close as we will ever get. Compared to this immediate presentation, the experience of succession as such, of past and future, is at best a faded recollection.

On the face of it, the successive style exemplified here serves to reinforce normal discursive awareness by appealing so strongly in its rhythmical presentation to the auditory sense. But the effect actually is just the reverse. Discursive reflection can shape itself only when it is informed and activated by sentences articulated hypotactically—where, that is, there is a discernible logical structure to their arrangement. This is not the case here; as we have seen, this passage contains no copulatives connecting one sentence to the next, and there is no attempt whatsoever at logical articulation. Without such connectives, the sentences are free to organize themselves without reference to time or to syntax in the imagination of the reader, in the mind's eye. Another way of putting this is that, given the absence of textual mortar, each successive moment of vision arranges itself within the circular compass of the reader's eye just as it was seen by the narrator during its re-creation. Their relation, as it was perceptibly in nature, is one of parts to the whole, not items in sequence. The irony here is that, though Emerson's substitutive style appears to underscore sequence, its psychological effect on the reader is to heighten the vividness and intensity of each moment of presentation. By, as it were, purifying the experience of succession, he in effect activates the power of the vision itself. As the syntactic structure dissolves, attention centers on the semantic content. This rhetorical purification of succession thus leads to a loosening of the constrictions of temporal experience and a revelation of pure significance.

It is true that Emerson wrote grandly of the "Rhetoric" he studied and practiced as "the Building of Discourse" and criticized writing which "squandered" its "profoundest thoughts, sublime images, [and] dazzling figures" in "an immethodical harangue." But arrange these gems systematically, each according to its proper setting, in a "natural rhetoric," and "behold! out of the quarry you have erected a temple, soaring in due gradation, turret over tower to heaven, cheerful with thorough-lights, majestic with strength, desired of all eyes." It is perhaps not surprising that the structural guidelines laid down in this 1837 blueprint sound strongly reminiscent of *Nature*'s organization: "let the question be asked—What is said? How many things? Which are they?" (JMN, V, 409). But the problem is that if you try the structure of Emerson's majestic temple too severely it begins to look more like a castle in the air. "Commodity" shades off into "Beauty," "Beauty" into "Discipline," and all three into "Idealism." The uses which beauty serves—to perception, to morality, to intellect—overlap considerably with those served by discipline—understanding, reason, and conscience—and all are taken up once again in the context of "Idealism." The moral lesson seems particularly ubiquitous, and this is because, in Emerson's own words, "Herein is especially apprehended the Unity of Nature—the Unity in Variety,—which meets us everywhere. All the endless variety of things make a unique, an identical impression."[9] From chapter to chapter, categories overlap and truths are repeated. This is because the basic lesson is the same. The poet in his imaginative apprehension of beauty and the philosopher in his intellectual grasp of truth appear to be aspiring to different goals, but in the end even their careers are seen to converge: "The true philosopher and the true poet are one, and a beauty, which is truth, and a truth, which is beauty, is the aim of both" (CW, I, 34). The largest distinction of all—that between nature and spirit—itself turns out to be merely an error of vision and an appearance only. All these departments and faculties are not sharply separated precincts of life but interpenetrating and overlapping values. It is the rhetorical framework that keeps them distinct, and not the nature of things. All particulars are constantly revolving about the One. Emerson's gradations, "turret over tower," are actually something of a facade. In reality, the whole apparent diversity is built out of thinner stuff.

There are moments in the unfolding of *Nature* when a circumspect reader cannot help but feel that he or she is caught up in a rhetoric of illusion, and this odd disparity between its self-circling argument and its apparently hierarchical structure certainly contributes to the raising of such suspicions. But this is not all that contributes to them: the essay as a whole is such an extraordinary mélange of rhetorical styles, tones, and voices that it is surprising we keep our bearings as well as we do. Indeed, *Nature*'s persona is so shifty, so elusive in its abandonment and adoption of alternative literary voices, that we might well wonder whether Emerson is not practicing here a kind of rhetorical ventriloquism. It is possible to go through the entire book marking at each juncture these abrupt and often unpredictable transitions in voice and style, but to make the point it will be enough simply to point out some of the most obvious such instances at the start.

Discounting the 1849 epigram, which complicates the introduction even more, we may note that the first paragraph already suggests *Nature*'s characteristic mixture of style and fluctuations of voice. The opening, beginning with the volley of sardonic declamation and proceeding with the famous rhetorical challenge ("Why should not we also enjoy an original relation to the universe?"), neatly exemplifies the hortatory style of an oratorical exordium. At the paragraph's midpoint, however, the momentum of this rousing oratory is unexpectedly slowed by an extended rhetorical question whose tone is surprisingly sensual and decidedly less challenging than the sentences leading up to it: "Embosomed for a season in nature, whose floods of life stream around and through us, and invite us by the powers they supply, to action proportioned to nature, why should we grope among the dry bones of the past, or put the living generation into masquerade out of its faded wardrobe?" As we have noted previously, this sentence is rife with biblical allusions and as such is at least partly indebted to pulpit rhetoric. But the modulation from a purely hortatory to a mixed homiletic style is somewhat odd here, as if the persona has without notice suddenly relaxed the vehemence and with it the public formality of the opening and begun addressing us in a rather more private and indeed sanguine tone.

Whatever the rhetorical affiliations of the first paragraph, they break off altogether with the introduction of the deceptively flat-footed assertion that begins paragraph 2. The tone here is matter-of-fact, but the contention obviously is not: "Undoubtedly we have no questions to ask which are unanswerable." This is the kind of sentence that gets Emerson into trouble with so many of his readers. What is the basis for such mild and facile confidence? It is the kind of writing that contributes to the caricature of Emerson as a disembodied eyeball. Either we doubt the integrity of this writer as a man in the world or wonder if he knows what he is talking about. But this is not the only instance of such disembodied rhetoric in *Nature;* it appears periodically throughout in the form of casually pointed irony ("To speak truly, few adult persons can see nature"), nonchalant philosophic hyperbole ("Intellectual science has been observed to beget invariably a doubt of the existence of matter"), parables (as in the Orphic chant), and most characteristically, aphorisms, such as the one embedded in the center of this paragraph: "Every man's condition is a solution in hieroglyphic to those inquiries he would put." What all these forms have in common is a disparity between what the persona of *Nature* means to say, which is often shrouded in mystery, and the way he says it, which is, at least apparently, casual and off-handed. Either the assertion is introduced under the guise of transparency, which it is not, or in the context of a simple and straightforward form such as the parable or apothegm. The name best given to this kind of presentation is wisdom rhetoric, in that it requires a definite act of discernment on the part of the reader to make the leap from apparently off-handed formulation to more recondite interpretation.

Having momentarily involved us in the mysteries of this second paragraph, *Nature*'s persona wastes no time suggesting their solution. Instead, as we have seen, he shifts immediately into a fourth rhetorical style, as we are led to a consideration of "a theory of nature." The tone of this section is of course academic; its discourse propositional; and its aim, apparently, instructive. We find ourselves in a completely different context of discourse and wonder how, after the first two paragraphs, we ever got there. This is not the last time we are to meet with such rhetoric—it dominates large parts of the sections on "Language," with its famous set of propositions, and "Idealism"; and we find features of its definitional style cropping up elsewhere as well: "This love of beauty is Taste. . . . The creation of beauty is Art" (CW, I, 16).

The ruse behind this rhetoric, as we have noted, becomes evident enough when we see that the subsequent treatment does not live up to its implied academic standards. What follows is not rational demonstration, as we were given to expect, but something rather different: "To go into solitude, a man needs to retire as much from his chamber as from society." Here we begin with a meditation on solitude that opens out into *Nature*'s famous panegyric on the stars. The sudden shift from pedagogical discourse to reverential witness—this move, without linguistic transition, from indoors to outdoors—leaves us feeling somewhat disoriented. Following Aristotle we might characterize this fifth form of discourse as epideictic or display rhetoric, and there are several examples of it in Emerson's appreciative descriptions of nature in his section on "Beauty" (CW, I, 13–14). Here, as there, its evocative prose arrests our attention and, in effect, encourages us to forget any possible bearing it might have on the dry propositional remarks which went before.

The next two paragraphs witness continuing tonal and stylistic fluctuation, from a rhetoric of aphorism ("Nature never wears a mean appearance"), back again to pedagogical discourse ("When we speak of nature in this manner, we have a distinct but most poetical sense in mind"), to the wisdom rhetoric which introduces the next paragraph. This last section provides, in effect, the preamble to the famous hierophany on the bare common whose presentation we analyzed in some detail in the last chapter. The passage in which the famous transparent eyeball appears is without question the most dramatic instance in *Nature* of what we would best identify as oracular rhetoric. Another vivid example occurs in "Spirit," which we will note further on (CW, I, 38). The distinctive feature of the style of Emerson's grotesque Self-revelation is that it seeks to annul our usual sense of a disjunction between being and speaking by annulling our sense of the disjunction between the narrator and his words. It is perhaps the most extreme manifestation of a rhetorical strategy that governs *Nature* at every turn. Such sentences are not really descriptive or expository at all, as Warner Berthoff has pointed out, but projective and performative.[10] The ostensible subject of this passage is an event that took place at some prior time on the bare common, but the real subject is the hierophantic formulation itself, which is designedly self-constituting. The meaning achieved here in formulation is the only meaning Emerson really cares about. By virtue of its bluntness and vigor, its shock of immediacy, this passage creates its subject originally under the pretense that it is only reenacting it from before.

With the announcement of the second chapter, we are presented with a discussion on "Commodity," and not surprisingly by now, the style of discourse shifts once again. Here we are treated to one of the clearest and most affecting examples of Emerson's use of catalogue rhetoric.[11] The chapter opens with a short organizational list and then proceeds to a rhapsodic survey of nature's beneficence:

What angels invented these splendid ornaments, these rich conveniences, this ocean of air above, this ocean of water beneath, this firmament of earth between? this zodiac of lights, this tent of dropping clouds, this striped coat of climates, this fourfold year? Beasts, fire, water, stones, and corn serve him. The field is at once his floor, his work-yard, his play-ground, his garden, and his bed. (CW, I, 11)

The style evinced here is a popular one with Emerson: like the forms of discourse we have just cited, we encounter bursts of it periodically throughout *Nature*.[12] It is no doubt one of the characteristic features of Whitman's own poetic style, which he owed in part to the man he referred to as "master." The effect on the reading experience of such extended catalogues is of course one of accelerated imaginative transport and, if we consider the dimensions of such sweeping surveys, also expansion. It is an exercise, we might say, in re-creative agility, insofar as this kind of reading engages the attention in quickened successions of apprehension and release, or mental contractions and expansion. As soon as the mind has entertained a new image, it must let it go for something new and unprecedented.

These lists function then as stimulants; taking up the tempo of Emerson's presentations, they shake the reader's attention out of its reading routines. The imaginative expansion that results, we might describe as metonymic: in contrast to symbolic presentations which center the attention, these runs of imagery stretch the boundaries of the mind laterally over the surface of the world. As we shall see, *Nature* as a whole seems to gravitate around its symbolic centers, its atoms of aphorism, but Emerson's evident fascination with his catalogues, even at this early stage in his writing career, suggests another crucial rhetorical strategy and a view of the imagination based more on flux than on stasis. This conception of the imagination, and its relation to the catalogue, finds suggestive justification in this passage from his later essay "Poetry and Imagination": "As the bird alights on the bough, then plunges into the air again, so the thoughts of God pause but for a moment in any form. All thinking is analogizing, and it is the use of life to learn metonymy. The endless passing of one element into

new forms, the incessant metamorphosis, explains the rank
which imagination holds in our catalogue of mental powers" (W,
VIII, 20). There is sometimes a tendency to skim *Nature*'s lists on
the assumption that their import may be just as easily suggested
through some general conception, but the distinctive feature of
most Emersonian catalogues, like those of Whitman's *Leaves,* is
that they cannot be generalized without destroying their whole
purpose. They are interesting to analyze not so much for what
they say to us as for what they do to us in the process of reading.

The seven styles described above by no means exhaust Emerson's rhetorical repertoire, as continued analysis would show:
there are also variants of a conversational style, an essayistic
style, a colloquial style. We find mixtures of genre and of discourse, as in the case of the Orphic song, which is part myth, part
parable, and part oracular chant (CW, I, 41–42). Also various are
the particular rhetorical devices themselves, especially irony, hyperbole, apostrophe, rhetorical questions, and shock tactics—not
to speak of the various grammatical and syntactic inconsistencies
which David Porter has neatly identified as characteristic of Emerson's prose style generally.[13]

For the reader the result of all these rhetorical shifts and feints is
a periodic sense of displacement, even disorientation, that seems
almost programmatic. There is no consistent rhetorical style in
Nature, no consistent voice. It appears rather to be the creation of
many voices or, perhaps better, a composite voice such as the "voice
of many waters" which, interestingly, we hear in the revelations of
Jeremiah and John of Patmos (Jer. 43.2; Rev. 14.2, 19.6). As in the
oracular rhetoric that epitomizes it, the effect of Emerson's protean
style, his romantic glossolalia, is to sever, or at least seriously to
complicate, the assumed relation between the text and its pre-
sumed author. Emerson, we realize by now, is not someone we will
ever know through *Nature:* the most we can know is his oracular
voice—clear, serene, multiplex, and mercurial—unmistakably
Emerson, but one of the strangest combinations of command and
dispassion anywhere in literature. At the least juncture of *Nature*'s
argument, just when we seem to be getting our bearings, its persona is apt to break off and leave us in suspension. As *Nature*'s
voice continues, we often find ourselves in a different world of

discourse, wakened to a fresh encounter, but tricked into a forgetfulness of how we arrived there.

The Reader's Apocalypse

If *Nature* lacks cohesion, it is obviously not because Emerson was
unable to think clearly. The reason lies as much with the sentences themselves as with the structure they help form. Here, as
many critics have noted, Emerson concentrates all the strength of
his prose: "If the stars should appear one night in a thousand
years, how would men believe and adore; and preserve for many
generations the remembrance of the city of God which had been
shown!" (CW, I, 8–9); "The health of the eye seems to demand a
horizon" (13); "Beauty is the mark God sets upon Virtue" (16); "A
work of art is an abstract or epitome of the world" (16); "Every
universal truth which we express in words, implies or supposes
every other truth" (28); "An action is the perfection and publication of thought" (28); "A man is a god in ruins" (42).[14] The sentence is the irreducible and irrefrangible unit of Emerson's writing, and if the several styles of discourse just cited have anything
in common, it is that they tend to gravitate around one or a few
strong sentences, whether they be aphorisms, apostrophes, descriptions, oracles, or rhetorical questions. Such sentences are the
hallmarks of Emerson's style; epitomizing for us his characteristic turn of mind, they are also indispensable to his rhetorical
program and his designs on us, his readers.

These "infinitely repellent particles," as he aptly referred to
them, resist transition and assimilation because they resist participation. The sentences of Emerson's essays are so highly con-
densed and polished that they seem to have acquired an integrity
and a will all their own. As in an atom, a jewel, or a plant, the
energy of Emerson's characteristic sentence is predominantly centripetal. And this fact also reflects the abiding reflexiveness of
Emerson's mind. "I fancy," he wrote to Carlyle, "I need more than

another to *speak* with such a formidable tendency to the lapidary style. I build my house of boulders" (CEC, 308).

Such mineral metaphors seem appropriate for characterizing not only the structure of Emerson's sentences but also their provenance. As any student of the Journals may verify, Emerson did not manufacture these jewels in the first sitting—he mined them. Many of his finest creations received their final shape only after years of evolution in the Journals. *Nature,* like many of the essays, represents a complex cross section of literary strata. The famous "crossing" passage analyzed previously results from the reworking of a series of journal entries extending from 1833 up to a few weeks before *Nature* was published (cf. CW, I, 270–71). But for other sections Emerson was by no means hesitant to dig as far back as the late twenties for proverbs, provocative ideas, and turns of phrase. It is the consequence of such literary mining that a formulation from some recent compositional period may be surrounded by others far older.

Emerson's extreme preoccupation with each sentence of the composition was more than enough to give it the appearance and feel of a mosaic whose facets cut a thousand ways. "Do they think the composition too highly wrought? A poem should be a blade of Damascus steel made up of a mass of knife blades and nails and parts every one of which has had its whole surface hammered and wrought before it is welded into the Sword to be wrought over anew" (JMN, V, 362). If Emerson's metaphor sounds excessively masculine, this is no accident. He liked his sentences for the same reason he liked certain men—for their robust self-reliance. It is interesting that the phrase "infinitely repellent" turns up in the Journals also, but here it is used not for sentences but for the individual man, *an* individual man—Emerson's blustery friend Bronson Alcott: "Here is Alcott by my door,—yet is the union more profound? No, the Sea, vocation, poverty, are seeming fences, but Man is insular, and cannot be touched. Every man is an infinitely repellent orb, and holds his individual being on that condition" (JMN, V, 329).

To Emerson such bluff independence might make for difficulties in the meeting of minds, but this was an unrealistic ideal anyhow. Independence was the anchor of personal nobility, in speech as well as action. Here especially is where Emerson's rhetoric invites a Bloomian reading. To be a man, he believed, is to resist the influence of the past, even if that influence is generated by the last sentence you wrote. One of Emerson's favorite literary models was Montaigne, and in this light we can begin to see better why: "Glad to read in my old gossip Montaigne some robust rules of rhetoric: I will have a chapter thereon in my book. I would Thomas Carlyle should read them. 'In good prose (said Schlegel (?)) every word should be underscored.' Its place in the sentence should make its emphasis. Write solid sentences and you can even spare punctuation" (JMN, IV, 273). So great was Emerson's assurance in the redeeming value of good sentences that he was completely unruffled when the first proof-sheet of *Nature* returned to him full of errors and indelicacies: "The peace of the author cannot be wounded by such trifles, if he sees that the sentences are still good. A good sentence can never be put out of countenance by any blunder of compositors. It is good in text or note, in poetry or prose, as title or corollary. But a bad sentence shows all his flaws instantly by such dislocation" (JMN, V, 190).

The sentence then was the reflection of the writer, a gauge of his character and will. If one sentence did not follow the rest, this was a flaw only if it lacked integrity within itself. Indeed, the greatest sentences, like the representative men, were justification unto themselves. Each created its own context, justified itself: "Every composition in prose or verse should contain in itself the reason of its appearance. Thousands of volumes have been written and mould in libraries of which this reason is yet to seek—does not appear. Then comes Adam Smith, Bacon, Burke, Milton, then comes any good sentence and its apology is its own worth. It makes its pertinence" (JMN, III, 280). If the sentences were sound, the virtue of the book would be secure. Organization, logic, system—these were trifling matters in comparison. This is why, apparently, Emerson was so lenient in his criticism of the evident disorder of Bacon's prose. Though his works are "fragmentary" and lack "a method derived from the Mind," he hives the wisdom of generations into his "massive sentences." To Emerson,

Bacon's writing is "a vast collection of proverbs," and this alone, despite the lack of organization, guarantees its value to posterity (EL, I, 320–36).

> Would you inspire in a young man a taste for Chaucer and Bacon? Quote them to him. Fear not to be like him who carried a tile as a sample of his palace; for the parallel does not hold unless the tile which the clown carried had been a diamond. It is a law of Wit that whoso can make a good sentence can make a good book. And to read a sentence of Hooker or Bacon is like offering a lump of gold as specimen of a mine or an apple to denote the quality of the tree; which would be right. Let the truths which we owe to Bacon and Taylor be communicated and let him judge of the writer not as a faultfinder but by the delight which is the proper attendant of great sentiments and profound observations. (EL, I, 214)

Whether in the Journals or his published works, Emerson's words, like Bacon's, tended to organize around the proverbial. Something more than the merely personal emerges from the crucible that crystallizes these pithy sayings. And the result is that their surfaces reflect a perennial truth. "The proverbs of all nations," he wrote, "are always the literature of Reason, or the statements of an absolute truth, without qualification. Proverbs, like the sacred books of each nation, are the sanctuary of the Intuitions" (CW, II, 63–64).

After providing us with a sampling of such proverbs in *Nature,* Emerson goes on to note that "what is true of proverbs, is true of all fables, parables, and allegories" (CW, I, 22). In all cases, the words configure or depict some moral or spiritual truth. These formulations are the tiles of the heavenly city made of substance all the same. In the Bible it is verbal units such as these that constitute the primary building blocks. Northrop Frye remarks that, in contrast to continuous or descriptive discourse which has a democratic appeal, biblical rhetoric consists largely of "a discontinuous prose of aphorisms or oracles in which every sentence is surrounded by a silence." The rhythm of the Bible, he suggests, expands from a series of such "kernels," or seed-sayings, which constitute the respective centers of each biblical book. So, in the Wisdom books, the kernel is in the form of proverbs or aphorisms; in the Prophets it is the oracle; in the Pentateuch it is the commandment; and in the Gospels it is the pericope.[15]

As Matthiessen has pointed out, Emerson's conception of the proverb has a good deal in common with Coleridge's conception of the aphorism.[16] Both see in the verbal formulation a picture which directly participates in the moral or spiritual reality it represents (EL, I, 24–25). Coleridge's *Aids to Reflection,* a work that Emerson studied carefully, was dedicated above all to directing the reader's attention "to the value of the science of words." For Coleridge words were not only "the vehicle of thought but the wheels," and it is no accident that Coleridge's lessons on the subject were presented in the form of a series of aphorisms with accompanying commentary. One such aphorism reflects explicitly upon itself: "Exclusively of the abstract sciences, the largest and worthiest portion of our knowledge consists of aphorisms and the greatest and best of men is but an aphorism." In the comment to a previous aphorism, Coleridge recommends the practice, "customary with religious men in former times," of taking up particular aphorisms for sustained "meditation." Conveniently, and for Coleridge's program here, consistently, the etymology of the word *aphorism* itself suggests the way in which such meditation ought to proceed. Here is the relevant note which he provides for the benefit of his reflective readers:

> *Aphorism,* determinate position, from the Greek *ap,* from; and *horizein,* to bound or limit; whence our horizon. In order to get the full sense of a word, we should first present to our minds the visual image that forms its primary meaning. Draw lines of different colours round the different countries of England, and then cut out each separately, as in the common play-maps that children take to pieces and put together—so that each district can be contemplated apart from the rest, as a whole in itself. This twofold act of circum-

scribing and detaching, when it is exerted by the mind on subjects of reflection and reason is to aphorize, and the result an aphorism.[17]

In respect at least to his penchant for etymologizing, Coleridge had no more enthusiastic disciple than Emerson himself, as *Nature*'s section on "Language" serves to show (CW, I, 18). But Emerson may have had another reason to pause long over this particular derivation. Charles Emerson, whose life and recent passing haunt *Nature* at several points, was, like his brother, fond of aphorisms. Witticisms and pithy observations communicated by Charles to his brother during their strolls around Concord turn up frequently in Waldo's Journals. But from one in particular Emerson appears to have drawn unusual significance; "You never are tired," observed Charles, "whilst you can see far" (JMN, IV, 255). In *Nature* Emerson conflates Charles's epigrammatic remark with an image of his own, in the process of elaborating an aphorism to suit *Nature*. Here in "Beauty" is its fuller context: "The tradesman, the attorney comes out of the din and craft of the street, and sees the sky and the woods, and is a man again. In their eternal calm, he finds himself. The health of the eye seems to demand a horizon. We are never tired, so long as we can see far enough" (CW, I, 13).

Emerson liked to look out onto the horizon. As Charles had maintained, it was a perspective of which he never tired. In it he sought the sum and invisible yield of all the proximate parts of nature. Indeed, horizon-gazing was the key to deciphering the sense underlying all particular times and places.

> The charming landscape which I saw this morning, is indubitably made up of some twenty or thirty farms. Miller owns this field, Locke that, and Manning the woodland beyond. But none of them owns the landscape. There is a property in the horizon which no man has but he whose eye can integrate all the parts, that is, the poet. This is the best part of these men's farms, yet to this their warranty-deeds give no title. (CW, I, 9)

What the horizon does of course is to circumscribe. It gives a holistic shape and smooth edge to all the jagged facts of the world. When we see to the horizon, we include those facts without being included by them. To comprehend the world, as we do when we gaze off to the horizon, is to transcend the world: it is a way of putting the world inside us, if only momentarily. To glimpse the horizons was for Emerson to glimpse the Orphic Man—before he shrank from his gigantic compass. In fact, this cognition of the limits of the world is not in its real import a cognition about nature at all; it is a cognition about the self. In seeing for the first time the rim of creation as boundary, the seer recognizes what he or she is not, fully and finally. But this cognition has no value compared to the one which tumbles in upon it—the connected realization of what he or she is. Emerson's meditations on the horizon epitomize his meditations on all the parts of nature: in the last analysis they all turn out to be meditations on the self, a fact attested by the otherwise anomalous conclusion of his central revelation on the bare common. "In the wilderness, I find something more dear and connate than in streets or villages. In the tranquil landscape, and especially in the distant line of the horizon, man beholds somewhat as beautiful as his own nature" (CW, I, 10).

Like *type, horizon* is a crucial word for our reading of *Nature*. Emerson returns to it several times. It is crucial because it translates his own meditation on nature to our reading of *Nature*. The twofold action of outward comprehension and inward self-reflection, which Emerson experiences in his gazing on the horizon, is parallel to the practice which Coleridge recommends for the study of aphorism in his *Aids to Reflection*. Whether or not Emerson remembered Coleridge's interesting footnote, it is clear that for the author of *Nature* meditation on the horizon is what generates the aphorism. To horizon is to aphorize—to circumscribe and encapsule a larger reality. It is primarily a way of seeing; indeed, horizoning is merely another expression of Emerson's distinctive "angle of vision." The eye encompasses the world until the world becomes the eye. This is what the poet, in fact, must accomplish; envisioning the world as a whole, he then

turns it back into the self. What results for the writer is momentary transfiguration, a glimpse in apocalypse; what results for
the reader is an aphorism, its earthly husk. Indeed, for the
reader this is all there is. Emerson's lovely crimson horizons are
for us no more than tropes and black marks on the page. But
what after all is the difference? Emerson's own horizons are
themselves immaterial. It is not really the tints of grandeur that
matter in the sunset and sunrise, since, as he suggests, it is all a
passing show; what matters is the vision that results. Emerson,
as we have seen, was never absorbed in the carnal sense of
nature's forms but always in their spiritual sense. He read into
nature, he did not merely behold it. Horizon was a trope from
the beginning—the literal sight serving merely as conveyance.
Gazing on the horizon in *Nature,* like all of Emerson's visions, is
a symbol, a figure of speech, which like Coleridge's aphorism
makes a particular claim on us.

What Emerson's horizon and Coleridge's aphorism have in common then is this englobing of reality. In all such language forms,
whether found in the Bible or among the proverbs and aphorisms
of writers such as Bacon, Montaigne, Coleridge, or Emerson,
meaning is completed in the self-referential. Significance is gath-
ered within the structure of the linguistic unit itself, not outside
of it. Susanne K. Langer has provided us with a helpful way of
distinguishing between these two types of communication in her
distinction between discursive and presentational symbolism.
"The meanings given through language," she writes,

> are successively understood, and gathered into a whole by
> the process called discourse; the meaning of all other sym-
> bolic elements that compose a larger, articulate symbol are
> understood only through the meaning of the whole, through
> their relations within the total structure. Their very func-
> tioning as symbols depends on the fact they they are in-
> volved in a simultaneous, integral presentation. This kind
> of semantic may be called "presentational symbolism," to
> characterize its essential distinction from discursive symbol-
> ism, or "language" proper.[18]

Langer's presentational symbolism is best characterized in terms of sensible objects, but this by no means limits its domain to nonverbal expression, as we shall see.

Discursiveness is perhaps no more characteristic of prose than it is of poetry, but it is more obvious there. We gather the significance of what we are reading word after word, sentence after sentence, paragraph after paragraph. In order to "follow" it, however, the reader must obviously do more than allow his eyes to drift across the page. Good reading is an active process. From the moment we begin to read, we begin to construct a significance of the text for ourselves. Prompted by various textual cues, the reader generates a second but responsive text, which is what we mean by the interpretation. This second meta-text is as much conditioned by the reader's own expectation, hypothesis formation, and past experience as by the signs on the page, but it is periodically brought into unison with the original text by a process of testing or verification, more or less rigorous depending on the character of the text and the disposition of the reader. The mechanics of this construction of significance by the reader and the dialogue which sustains it have been carefully elucidated in recent theories of aesthetic response, and to review these findings here would take us too far out of our orbit.[19] What is important to note for our purposes is that discursive prose by its very nature serves to establish and reinforce a disjunction defined by the interpretation of the reader and the text of the writer. The continual referencing between one and the other encourages a sustained dialogue which depends upon this ongoing relationship. To read such discursive texts, consequently, takes time. Their semantic structure can only entertain what Wolfgang Iser refers to as a "wandering viewpoint," since, unlike sensible objects or artistic forms which are presented all at once, the verbal meaning must necessarily be grasped only in stages. And this, of course, necessitates the preservation of a lively memory, since to understand the significance of what happens now, we must hold in remembrance what was said before. There is, we could say, a necessary delay between the encounter with discursive language and the later apprehension of its significance, as well as a continually renewed and projected anticipation.

The basic effect of discursive prose then is to create and affirm the relationship and separation between the reader and the text. Because this relationship requires continual verification by the reader against the textual cues, the text tends to remain at the center of the reader's activity. Discursive writing has sometimes been characterized as appealing to the consensus of its readership for adjudication, but there is a basic sense in which it refuses to yield its privileged authority. While allowing for a limited freedom of interpretation, most texts maintain a continual pressure and constraint on the reader's response. The text always holds the reader to a more or less preconditioned range of interpretations.

This is not to say that as a writer Emerson did not have specific designs on us, his readers. In fact, in one sense, he is the most willful of writers. But his control is of a different order. He is not so much concerned to influence what we read as how we read, not the content of our knowledge so much as the state in which we apprehend such content. The force of Emerson's authorial control is to engage us, and then to free us from the compulsions of his words out of regard for our own interpretive power. One of the means he uses to achieve this objective is a deliberate suspension of interpretive constraints. It is precisely this lack of textual confirmation and control that many readers find so exasperating about Emerson's essayistic style. To some, perhaps, he abandons responsibility along with control. But then what can you expect from a prose which so often appears to start all over again with each period? If our recognition of Emerson's penchant for proverb and aphorism suggests anything at all, it is that he was benignly indifferent to the value of ordinary discursive communication. Notwithstanding all the expository pretense of *Nature,* does he not wind up at the culmination of his "argument" dismissing altogether the value of propositional language for ultimate knowledge? "We can foresee God in the course and, as it were, distant phenomena of matter; but when we try to define and describe himself, both language and thought desert us, and we are as helpless as fools and savages. That essence refuses to be recorded in propositions, but when man has worshipped him intellectually, the noblest ministry of nature is to stand as the apparition of God" (CW, I, 37). This is not to deny that we read over wide tracts of *Nature* discursively or that we read Emerson's sentences in more or less the same fashion, left to right, one after the other, as we do *Pilgrim's Progress*. But it is to suggest that *Nature*'s grainy texture is no accident and that it invites a different response from the reader than the more continuous rhetoric to which we are accustomed.

Emerson writes, deliberately and constitutionally, to frustrate a habitually discursive reading. The sentences call attention to themselves, not to their successors and predecessors. They were not composed to yield up their meaning passively, for the meaning is wound tightly into the sentence structure. We pause before these linguistic citadels in spite of our usual reading habits. And that is as it should be, because here it is the architecture itself which is part of the point. Many of Emerson's famous sentences, like Coleridge's aphorisms, or the various sorts of biblical "seed-sayings" noted by Frye, are sufficient unto themselves. By virtue of such formal indebtedness, Emerson's sentences aim at echoing biblical and other traditional authority, but the echo becomes an increasingly indistinguishable resonance as the form comes to be fully appropriated. While these sentences unfold themselves to the attention successively like any other sentence, their autonomy suggests a circular rather than a linear archetype. Like the horizon, the words of the aphorism complete a closed ring of significance. In *Nature,* as I have suggested in another context, such spherical structures are part of the sense. What this complementary relationship between structure and sense suggests is that, while we read Emerson's sentences discursively, we must apprehend them as wholes. Individual words look inward and obey the higher law of the sentence form. The result of Emerson's high-compression composition then is that his sentences turn into symbols. Like the symbols of which Coleridge famously wrote in *Aids to Reflection* and *The Statesman's Manual*, Emerson's most characteristic sentence is "tautegorical," participating in the meaning which "it renders intelligible."[20]

It is not, after all, surprising that *Nature* should be represented this way—as a constellation of symbols—because this is precisely the way, according to Emerson, the first book was written. The second and third propositions of "Language," *Nature*'s section of self-reference, state respectively that "particular natural facts are symbols of particular spiritual facts" and that "nature is the symbol of spirit" (CW, I, 17). The basic linguistic units of the original book, nature itself, were also symbols, were tautegorical, and ought to be read as such: "Every particle in nature, a leaf, a drop, a crystal, a moment of time is related to the whole, and partakes of the perfection of the whole. Each particle is a microcosm, and faithfully renders the likeness of the world" (CW, I, 27).

Nature's sentences, like the words of nature, are thus encyclopedic, small models that contain the wholes. This is why sequence and succession do not matter so much. One sentence, properly aphorized and represented, contains the whole story, if only we could read it finely enough. Properly read, *Nature* is a system of infinite correlation in which every facet reflects all the rest; part responds to part and all partake of the whole. Emerson's revelation then is not presented in the form of a series of statements or propositions about something else. It is self-representing. *Nature* is a book of symbols which crystallize from sentences, given the proper concentration of reading. In this respect also, it is very like the biblical Revelation to which it is partially indebted.

Though Emerson's rhetoric appears discursive enough, this is largely a facade. Its relative indifference to any principle of sequence suggests that it actually conforms more closely to what Langer referred to as "presentational symbolism." This kind of symbolism, the range of what I have been calling the "symbol" proper, is distinct from discursive communication in that it overcomes narrative time. Such symbols, according to Langer, are "involved in a simultaneous, integral presentation."[21] By abolishing the waiting period between the presentation of the linguistic sign and the apprehension of its significance, which we find in reading most novels, for instance, the symbol cancels ordinary time. The whole significance now hangs on the immediate presentation and only there. In a symbolic text such as *Nature,* if you do not grasp the significance of *any* symbolic representation, then you do not grasp the full significance of anything at all, and if you do even for one only, then you do for all. Here the temporal distinction between *kairos* and *chronos* revived by Frank Kermode helps to characterize the difference between the narrative and the symbolic consciousness. *Chronos* is "passing" or "waiting time." Narrative is that form of communication which generates and conditions it. Symbol, on the other hand, destroys duration in favor of immediate cognition. The time arising in this flash of significance is *kairos,* "a point in time filled with significance."[22] This is the time of the Apocalypse, when history has been consummated.

In chronological time we pay attention to what has been heard and remembered. We resign ourselves to the separation which has been established between ourselves and the source of inspiration in antiquity. This is the time in which *Nature* begins, retrospectively. But when revelation breaks in, all distance and duration suddenly dissolve. We *see* the significance. We are no longer mere auditors, passive recipients of experience; we are the seers. This is why the eye, and not the ear, is the reigning sense of *Nature,* and why vision is the metaphor of transcendence. In *Nature* we do not so much read across time as into it. The logic of Emerson's rhetoric is vertical, not horizontal, which is why he revises biblical typology in representing nature as symbol. "Idealism sees the world in God. It beholds the whole circle of persons and things, of actions and events, of country and religion, not as painfully accumulated, atom after atom, act after act, in an aged creeping Past, but as one vast picture, which God paints on the instant eternity, for the contemplation of the soul" (CW, I, 36).

The symbolic structure of *Nature*'s rhetoric naturally places special demands on the reader. If we are to make sense of it, we need to adjust our normal reading habits. Insofar as the center of meaning lies within the structure of the individual sentence and not somewhere down along the line of text, we have to linger a little in our reading. We should hear with the eyes as well as the ears, as if circling around each aphorism until we see how the aphorism circles around the world. In this reading it is not what we remember of what went before that is important. Memory lapses as the boundaries of the attention organize around the new structure in view. What we are called upon to see here is how all the parts of meaning are related to the whole vision simultaneously. This is not something we can figure out; it must be seen. And to see in this way—to see simultaneity—the discursive intellect must be momentarily abandoned. Analysis must be transcended in favor of a patient and sometimes sustained contemplation. Review and recapitulation are not symptoms necessarily of flagging attention but necessary means to glimpse the wider ramifications of what is being said. Attention must stop and center before moving on. This style of reading we might term periodic in order to emphasize the meditative space which must surround the otherwise consecutive movement of the discursive understanding.

Just as the symbolic structure of *Nature* helps to overcome the temporal divorce between sign and significance through the annulment of narrative time, so this periodic reading helps to overcome the more fundamental alienation between the text and the reader. Emerson's sentences are imperious, but they are not in any sense coercive. They do not restrain us or keep tabs on the ongoing interpretation. We either see the significance, in which case the illumination is its own proof, or we do not. If we do not, nothing further can be said. The only test of validity Emerson seemed much concerned with was the self-evident. "Whenever a true theory appears," he forewarned, "it will be its own evidence" (CW, I, 8). Indeed, Emerson was habitually distrustful of any claim which looked obsequiously elsewhere for legitimization, especially religious truth claims: "The truth of truth consists in this, that it is self-evident, self-subsistent. It is light. You don't get a candle to see the sun rise" (JMN, IV, 45).

When the heat of the reader's attention reaches a critical point, the aphorism begins to glow and turn translucent. Here is where the reader's apocalypse begins. The division between text and reader dissolves as the text sacrifices itself in the cognition of pure significance. This is the state of vision in which Reason and the world intermingle. Emerson believed the Book of Nature could be read this way and apprised us of the process: "A life in harmony with nature . . . will purge the eyes to understand her text. By degrees we may come to know the primitive sense of the permanent objects of nature, so that the world shall be to us an open book, and every form significant of its hidden life and final cause" (CW, I, 23). Carlyle insisted that objects of nature were windows into which the "philosophic eye" could view "Infinitude itself." "Where is that cunning eye and ear," declaims Teufelsdröckh, "to whom that God-written apocalypse will yield articulate meaning?"[23] Here also the burden is laid on the reader.

The apocalypse begins at the point where words and meanings are everywhere estranged, and ends in absolute transparency. Emerson hoped that one day his own book might be read this way and cared little that when it was the book itself would thereby be rendered disposable. *Nature* is vehicular; it is perhaps the supreme case in American literature of that mode of ministerial writing which strives to subordinate or dissolve itself in the process of fulfilling its distinctive pastoral aims. When Emerson's book is unsealed, his words become transparent. The reader is left reading from the Self only as his primary text, without the aid of Emerson's commentary. In narrative or ordinary discursive prose, the reader revolves around the text; in *Nature* the text revolves around the reader.

Part of the reason that *Nature*'s illusion of structure does not always sustain close inspection is that the mortar itself is a little porous: the bricks are lined with air. Emerson's writing reflects consummate sophistication and polish in all but one interesting respect—its transitions. Most accomplished essayists draw on a more or less varied repertoire of connecting words and concepts: but, because, although, since, unless, until, provided, and so forth. Emerson does not. He strings his sentences and paragraphs together with little more help than a few crude or specious copulatives—"and," "or"—if he bothers at all.

We have already seen several illustrations of this feature of his style, but here again it is exemplified perhaps most dramatically in the context of those passages we might best describe as oracular. Besides the "crossing" passage, the most vivid example of this sort of rhetoric occurs in "Spirit," to which *Nature*'s persona turns for the fulfillment of Idealism. In the final analysis, we will remember, the Ideal theory turns out to be incomplete, insofar as "it does not satisfy the demands of the spirit. It leaves God out of me" (CW, I, 37). The purpose of the penultimate chapter then is to complete *Nature*'s vision by locating God in the human heart, as well as in the world, and the oracle we turn to for the final revelation of the God within is appropriately enough "the recesses of consciousness" (CW, I, 38):

But when, following the invisible steps of thought, we come
to inquire, Whence is matter? and Whereto? many truths
arise to us out of the recesses of consciousness. We learn that
the highest is present to the soul of man, that the dread
universal essence, which is not wisdom, or love, or beauty, or
power, but all in one, and each entirely, is that for which all
things exist, and that by which they are; that spirit creates;
that behind nature, throughout nature, spirit is present;
that spirit is one and not compound; that spirit does not act
upon us from without, that is, in space and time, but spiritu-
ally, or through ourselves. Therefore, that spirit, that is, the
Supreme Being, does not build up nature around us, but
puts it forth through us, as the life of the tree puts forth new
branches and leaves through the pores of the old. (CW, I, 38)

The description here of the manner in which "truths arise"
from out of these "recesses of consciousness" suggests that the
inquiry inaugurated by the questions "Whence . . ." and "Whereto" moves along a vertical and not a horizontal axis of discovery.
The "invisible steps of thought" then are methodical only in an
apparent sense—what Emerson is really suggesting by this metaphor is the mystical ladder. Only here we do not *ascend* the
ladder as the patriarch Jacob did; rather we descend into consciousness upon its rungs. There is evidence of Emerson's revisionary concern even here, but in both cases, upward and downward, the result is the same—a revelation of the transcendent.
What is striking about this revelation of the God within, though,
is how effortless it is: a few downward steps, a couple of simple
questions, and the truths gush up in a fountain of cognitions.
This is revelation under pressure, insights in profusion. The
heart of the revelation of course is the unity of being, but it
comes to us in a torrent of subordinate clauses, all predicated on
the short, expeditious independent clause "We learn . . ." How do
we learn? The answer is all at once. Here again it would be
difficult to identify from our own standpoint the logic underlying
this successive presentation of clauses. Even the "therefore" that
culminates the oracle has an illusory logical sense insofar as all
it really introduces is yet another restatement or summary of

the series of cognitions that just preceded it. The tone here is of palpable enthusiasm, perhaps even ecstasy: *Nature*'s persona is beside himself, once again suggesting to us the sense that the words uttered here are performative—both self-generating and self-propelled. So overwhelming are these revelations from within that they appear to tumble over each other in their syntactical arrangement. Each clause presses behind the one preceding it, or squeezes itself in parenthetically, with such impatient force as to preclude almost entirely the imposition of coordinating conjunctions, other connectives, or full stops. The impression we get here is that there is no question of pausing to set up a new sentence: the revelation insists on instant expression, a formulation without delays. Indeed the oracle manages to discharge itself almost entirely into the extending confines of one sentence, punctuated only, and as if hastily, by a glut of commas and semicolons.

Here again we see the primacy of the sentence in Emerson's rhetoric, and with it a remarkable instance of the kind of syntactical discontinuity that so often comes in its wake. For the most part, Emerson seems to have remained completely unrepentant of this discontinuous tendency in his style, but sometimes he too found it a bit vexing. While preparing his first book of essays, he complained to Carlyle that it seemed but a "little raft" consisting of "only boards and logs tied together" (CEC, 291). Indeed, in this respect there is something a little primitive about Emerson's prose—but then that perhaps is part of the point.

Equipped with the right joints and rivets, the philosopher raises his verbal structures to the skies. Emerson pretended to do this, but his real habitation, where he felt most natural and did his best work, was much closer to the ground. "I dot evermore in my endless journal, a line on every unknowable in nature; but the arrangement loiters long, and I get a brick kiln instead of a house" (CEC, 278).[24] From his side Carlyle could only agree. It was the connective tissue in these essays that he found lacking. Emerson's sentences do not "rightly stick to their foregoers and their followers: the paragraph [is] not as a beaten *ingot,* but as a beautiful square *bag of duck-shot* held together by canvas!" (CEC, 371).

In his seminal study *The Act of Reading,* Wolfgang Iser has directed our attention to the crucial role played in texts by their communicative "gaps" or "indeterminacies." No communication, he argues, is ever without its penumbra of uncertainty. We cannot positively know the effects our words have on another person's mind. But if there exists a certain irreducible inexperienceability between two speakers, the apparent communication between text and reader is even more troubled with indeterminacy. Every text is unevenly communicative: what it says is a small portion to what it cannot say, and in the very act of expression it conceals more than it reveals. Ironically enough, for Iser it is the gap that allows the only real communication between text and reader to take place, because it is at this point that the text draws the reader into itself, prompting him or her to constitute its significance: "it is the elements of indeterminacy that enable the text to 'communicate' with the reader, in the sense that they induce him to participate both in the production and the comprehension of the work's intention."[25] By projecting his or her own significance into the open pores of the text, the reader creates the only meaning it will ever have. And the sparser the narrative, as Eric Auerbach has shown in his analysis of the sacrifice of Isaac, the more involving the action.[26]

Yet with all due respect to the biblical narrative, there is hardly a sparser text than *Nature.* The sentences are mere points compared to the space that stretches between them. Once again, Alcott provides the aptest analogy: "Each period is self-poised; there may be a chasm of years between the opening passage and the last written, and there is endless time in the composition. Jewels all! separate stars. You may have them in a galaxy, if you like, or view them separate and apart."[27] So enigmatic is this style that *Nature* is at times all but dissolved in indeterminacy. It is the common medium from which each expression arises and into which each expression subsides. The difference, however, between these gaps in *Nature* and the ones which, for example, Iser notes in the eighteenth-century novel is that *Nature*'s gaps are not conditional. The projection elicited by an indeterminacy of plot is subject to the modifications and control of subsequent narrative. In a symbolic text, in which each sentence or aphorism constitutes a re-created whole, there is no such control. The reader is on his own. The significance of *Nature*'s gaps is final, though repeated *ad infinitum*. Insofar as the text's presentations stand on their own, no amount of recall or foresight will help elucidate their meaning. What it demands is a continually renewed attention. In fact, we are better off abandoning our usual habits of reading. *Nature* is not a conventional text and cannot be understood by reading routinely. Every sentence begins all over again. Nothing of the past or future was meant to condition this revelation, and that is why it is organized in this way.

The kind of attention such reading requires is a rare thing even among the best and most devoted of readers. It will result only when the reader learns to recollect his or her mind fully for each subsequent sally of attention. And vital to such self-recollection is a continual process of mental clearance. To be fully available in each act of attention, consciousness must repeatedly free itself from the determinations of the past as well as the projections for the future. Recollection depends on forgetting, just as creation depends on clearance. Constant purification of the attention engenders the freshness and responsiveness necessary for the fuller apprehension of *Nature*'s sentences. The reading Emerson enjoins on us, therefore, is one of a progressive forgetting. The gap that stretches between one sentence and the next throws the mind back upon its own resources. In that moment of transition the text of *Nature* is as if destroyed and the subtext of the Self is revealed: forgetfulness results thereby in Self-recollection. The next sentence sets the stage for further apocalypse. Here in the gaps then is where the real reading, the revelation of *Nature,* takes place. The most significant feature of this rhetoric is the way it consumes or destroys itself in the gaps between one semantic unit and the next. It is by virtue of such gaps and rhetorical shifts that Emerson can inaugurate the apocalypse which he has envisioned in the minds of his readers. But this effect is not achieved by contrived opacity or literary nonchalance: Emerson's rhetoric is structured from its inception by the principles and practice of Self-reliance.

In her interesting recent analysis, Julie Ellison helps us to see in Emerson's prose style a continual dramatization of his preoccupation with independence and self-actualization. Each essay constitutes a kind of literary battlefield upon which the forces of influence and invention are constantly contending. Emerson's treatment of the strong voices of the past becomes a kind of progressive interpretation which ends by subsuming them to himself. The result, she argues, is not secondary criticism but a "poetry of analysis."

While Ellison may over-emphasize the interpersonal character of such antagonism in Emerson, she demonstrates for us the close integration between the man and his writing style. There is nothing arbitrary or purely idiosyncratic about this relation—it is unavoidable, and Emerson himself tells us so: "A man's *style* is his intellectual Voice only in part under his controul. It has its own proper tone and manner which when he is not thinking of it, it will always assume. He can mimic the voices of others, he can modulate it with the occasion and the passion, but it has its own individual nature."[28] But as we have seen, the most revealing feature of Emerson's rhetoric is not its characteristic "tone or manner," but the ways in which it reflects and induces the expressive and reflexive movements of consciousness identified in the previous chapter. This is not to say that his rhetoric reveals so much *what* Emerson thinks, since that is subject to constant change. Rather it reveals *how* he thinks—his characteristic rhythm of mind.

Emerson's is a pulsating prose: each sentence an expansion; the conceptual space before and after, its contractions. From the unmanifest represented at each period, the new sentence erupts without warning. Here, for example, is how Alcott described the suspense and novelty of Emerson's prose style:

> Even his hesitancy between the delivery of his periods, his perilous passages from paragraph to paragraph of manuscript, we have almost learned to like, as if he were but sorting his keys meanwhile for opening his cabinets; the spring of locks following, himself seemingly as eager as any of us to get sight of his specimens as they come forth from their proper drawers, and we wait willingly till his gem is out glittering; admire the setting, too, scarcely less than the jewel itself.[29]

This rhythm of rhetoric, this pulsation of expression and silence, is what we mean by self-reliance. And if Emerson's rhetoric occasions a self-reliant reading, it is partly because these were the mechanics by which it was structured in composition. "A meek self reliance," he wrote in 1835, is "the law and constitution of good writing" (JMN, V, 92). The impulses of the pen correspond to the pulsations of the mind. What the reader finds himself doing in the reading of this text, the author did in its writing. The rhetorical structure itself gives testimony to the mechanics of its origin and inaugurates in the reader their recapitulation. While the creation of this rhetoric may not be fully subject to conscious control, that does not mean it is not sanctioned by conscious concern. Emerson's rhetoric reveals his mind, but it is deployed in the willful complicity of his stratagems as writer and teacher.

It is the peculiar distinction of this rhetoric, however, that it reveals the dynamics of this mind without revealing many of its judgments. Emerson has in effect completely abandoned the classical motive of rhetoric, which was above all to persuade, while nevertheless availing himself of much of its armory of strategies and devices. We can never be sure what the author of *Nature* or the essays really believes, and what he just experiments with. As we have noted with regard to *Nature*'s abrupt rhetorical shifts, Emerson's rhetoric is thoroughly ironic.[30] Sudden alterations in tone leave us in doubt as to where the writer or his persona really stands. In *Nature*'s gaps and lapses, the author seems to have gone into hiding—a kind of authorial *deus absconditus*. The sense of the author's presence appears and disappears with the periodic presentation and dissolution of his sentences. In *Nature* Emerson is a kind of pulsatory presence, and we are never sure he will mean the same to us this time as the last. As a consequence of his ironic and self-destructive rhetoric, the author continually evades his readers. Whitman, we remember, subscribed to a personal theory of poetry; he aspired to place himself, as he said, "freely, fully, and truly on record." Behind *Leaves of Grass* is a man, a contradictory, even an elusive man, to be sure; but behind *Nature* there is nothing but unfathomable ironic space. As the writer of *Nature*, Emerson is as much a sphinx as the nature he ironically professed to represent.[31]

The evasiveness of *Nature*'s author is partly attributable to the fluctuations and oscillations of his mind. But such evasiveness is not without method. No prose is more self-conscious or more calculated than Emerson's. If he aims to lead his readers away from himself, it is only so that he can lead them back toward themselves. It was a strategy he adhered to all his life: "The great always introduce us to facts; small men introduce us always to themselves. The great man, even whilst he relates a private fact personal to him, is really leading us away from him to an universal experience" (J, XII, 313).[32] Informing Emerson's conception of the great teacher is his paradigmatic conception of artistic and religious inspiration; and informing his conception of the self-effacing writer, as I suggested in chapter 2, is the self-denying worshipper and, ultimately, the kenotic Christ. As readers we are brought back to ourselves fully only when we are willing to sacrifice our prior understandings. Emerson believed this and knew that the reader's revelation depended therefore on the author's own voluntary and deliberate self-negation. The reader comes into full consciousness only when the author recedes into the calculated gaps and indeterminacies of the text.

In *Nature* then the burden of significance rests squarely upon the reader. No reading could be more demanding than this, since so much is required and so much is at stake. But there is also an assuredness that comes in this reading when the mind begins to move according to the rhythms of the rhetoric. Here is the fulfillment of *Nature*'s design; this above all is what we were meant to see. For our interpretation we have no constant authority but ourselves to appeal to; and except for that recognition *Nature* provides no further sanctions.

5 The Marriage Celebrated

From the standpoint of church history, Emerson is generally regarded as a radical, if not revolutionary, figure. He is situated, not without justification, at the far left of Protestantism, if not off the spectrum of Christian denominations altogether. While such placement may be valid with respect to Christian doctrine, it is an oversimplification with respect to Christian piety. Indeed, the net force of this book suggests, in a way which runs at times contrary to current scholarly opinion, that in important ways Emerson was a deeply conservative religious thinker. In no regard is this more apparent than in his attitudes about inspired texts and his views on their reading and interpretation.

Emerson may have been the product of a Protestant tradition, but he favored none of the literalism characteristic of much Protestant exegesis of the Bible since the time of Luther. In this he was even more latitudinarian than the well-educated and urbane Unitarians of his father's generation. But, as we have seen in regard to his early attitude to the question of miracles, Emerson did not so much reject the literal historical sense as reinterpret it. It was not, after all, the outer meaning that made a book like the Bible valuable, but its inner meaning. Indeed, any book worth its salt required labor before it would divulge its interior significance. A good book consisted of layers of meaning, from concrete to abstract, which corresponded to increasingly subtle levels in the consciousness of the reader. While Emerson may at times have felt a little genuine Protestant and Yankee restlessness when he visited Saint Peter's in 1833, he would have had little trouble with the traditional Catholic approach to biblical interpretation.[1] He never espoused or methodically practiced a multileveled method of interpretation such as that adopted by Augustine or Thomas Aquinas, but his own attitude to the interpretation of inspired texts owes much more to the spirit of allegorical and mystical interpretation formulated by the Church Fathers and filtered down into the esoteric wisdom cults of the Renaissance than it does to Protestant exegesis. It was this kind of reading, gravitating always to the mystical core of the text, that attracted him so much to esoteric exegetes such as Boehme and Swedenborg, however unorthodox their particular interpretations.

Though by no means restricted to Christian, or even Judeo-Christian, exegesis, the tradition that sees in the text an interior spiritual sense is orthodox and widely catholic. It is the way, according to one defensible reading, that several New Testament texts understand themselves. In the second letter to the Corinthians, Saint Paul relies on apocalyptic language when he acknowledges that the gospel of Jesus Christ is hidden or "veiled" (2 Cor. 4.3). This conception of a secret gospel is also picked up by the synoptic writers and provides the basis for one of the most intriguing and disconcerting remarks anywhere in the New Testament on the issue of interpretation:

> And when he was alone, they that were about him with the twelve asked of him the parable. And he said unto them, Unto you it is given to know the mystery of the Kingdom of God; but unto those who are outside, all these things are done in parables, That seeing they may see, and not perceive; and hearing they may hear, and not understand; lest at any time they should be converted, and their sins should be forgiven them. (Mk. 4.10–12)

As Frank Kermode has adroitly shown, such hermeneutical separation of the sheep from the goats is not limited to religious texts. Most works of interpretation—of literary as well as religious texts—tend to set up a division between the insider, who is privy to the real significance, and the outsider, who is not. This is partly attributable to the nature of the text itself, which necessarily conceals as much as it reveals, and partly attributable to the perennial if futile hope which feeds all interpretive activity that somehow, somewhere, the "true" meaning can be penetrated and the secret glimpsed.[2] Whether or not we accept Kermode's "cheerless conclusion" that all such aspirations end finally and inevitably in disappointment, it is clear that for the biblical writers the implications of one's interpretation are grave indeed. Right understanding signifies membership in the Kingdom of Heaven; wrong understanding signifies damnation. The parable acts as a gate which swings one way to admit the elect and the other to debar all the rest. Interpretation does not take place in isolation from the interpreter's existential status but is a reflection and gauge of it.[3]

While Emerson impatiently jettisoned the invidious dogma of divine election and all its eschatological apparatus, the secret gospel idea was implicit in his whole way of thinking about all significant texts and their interpretation. It naturally followed from his bookish way of looking at things that nature itself would turn out to be the most secretive and seductive of all such texts. Her significance would always outrun the cognitions of even the bravest of speculators:

> The stars awaken a certain reverence, because though always present, they are always inaccessible; but all natural objects make a kindred impression, when the mind is open to their influence. Nature never wears a mean appearance. Neither does the wisest man extort all her secret, and lose his curiosity by finding out all her perfection. Nature never became a toy to a wise spirit. The flowers, the animals, the mountains, reflected all the wisdom of his best hour, as much as they had delighted the simplicity of his childhood. (CW, I, 9)

The Book of Nature then consists of innumerable layers of sense, from literal to abstract, and it takes the proper interpreter to explore its subtler phases. When this is the case for the paragon of texts, it is not then surprising to find such a multiplex semantic structure in the writings of great men also. "A man cannot bury his meanings so deep in his book, but time and like-minded men will find them. Plato had a secret doctrine, had he? What secret can he conceal from the eyes of Bacon? of Montaigne? of Kant? Therefore, Aristotle said of his works, 'They are published and not published' " (CW, II, 85). The fact that the first sentence of this citation was drawn from the journals of the summer in which Emerson was finalizing *Nature* suggests that he had such a structure in his designs also (JMN, V, 184). What it shows to us, however, is that the depth is less a function of the text than of the reader's consciousness. Texts themselves do not conceal; it is readers who overlook. All meanings are transparent, only it takes an eye sharp enough to see them so. This Emerson clarifies for us in the paragraph that follows his comment on books and their secret doctrines:

> No man can learn what he has not preparation for learning, however near to his eyes is the object. A chemist may tell his most precious secrets to a carpenter, and he shall be never the wiser,—the secrets he would not utter to a chemist for an estate. God screens us evermore from premature ideas. Our eyes are holden that we cannot see things that stare us in the face, until the hour arrives when the mind is ripened; then we behold them, and the time when we saw them not, is like a dream.

This formulation of a necessarily obscured vision echoes the divinely sanctioned obfuscation of Mark 4, but Emerson has given it a rather more benign and natural twist. We cannot see things that stare us in the face because it would be premature and, by implication, unhealthy for us to do so. Emerson softens the apparent arbitrariness of divine election by substituting a kind of developmental hermeneutics. There are still good readers and bad readers, insiders and outsiders, but this is not a consequence of a rigidly fixed divine fiat but a natural expression of spiritual growth. Here in "Spiritual Laws" the apocalyptic phrasing and tone still survive, but the judgment is easier to accept. Books are unsealed and secrets revealed in a natural way when the eye itself reaches sufficient ripeness. To Emerson the existence of such mature readers was an article of faith, and their enlightened reading was the hope and salvation for any good book. When in his journals of 1835, he exhorted himself to "mend Montaigne" and write his own essays, he ended with this question, "Can you not write as though you wrote to yourself and drop the token assured that a wise hand will pick it up?" (JMN, V, 40).

While Emerson relaxes the harshness of Saint Mark's hermeneutical election, he does not by any means increase the ranks of the elect readership. By all accounts the true reader is a rare soul indeed. A deep book may linger for centuries before it finds the wise one destined to understand it. When it finally does so, it comes full circle, since in the apprehension of such a reader it is as if inspired all over again.

> A good book is like the Ancient Mariner who can tell his tale only to a few men destined to hear it. It passes by thousands and thousands but when it finds a true reader it enters into him as a new soul. A good reader is rare. As we say translations are rare because to be a good translator needs all the talents of an original author so to be a good reader needs the high qualities of a good writer. Reading must not be passive. The pupil must conspire with the Teachers. It needs Shakspear, it needs a Bacon, to read Shakspear and Bacon in the best manner. (EL, I, 214)

Emerson's emphasis throughout his writings on the crucial role of the reader arises from his radical epistemological conviction that there is no textual meaning independent of the consciousness of the reader. Blake wrote that "the Sun's Light when he unfolds it depends on the Organ that beholds it." Emerson would have agreed; he applied the same principle to the reading of books.

> What's a book? Everything or nothing. The eye that sees it is all. What is the heavens' majestical roof fretted with golden fire to one man, but a foul and pestilent congregation of vapors. Well a book is to a paddy a fair page smutted

over with black marks; to a boy, a goodly collection of
words he can read; to a halfwise man, it is a lesson which
he wholly accepts or wholly rejects; but a sage shall see in
it secrets yet unrevealed. (JMN, V, 93)

His views on reading led Emerson precipitously close to a kind
of literary solipsism. In 1832, for instance, he drafted an entry
into his journal that could hardly be called anything else: "What
can we see, read, acquire, but ourselves? Cousin is a thousand
books to a thousand persons. Take the book, my friend, and read
your eyes out; you will never find there what I find" (JMN, III,
327). The book, we could say, is structured in the consciousness of
the reader. It comes into being here or not at all. Though we may
encounter the words, we cannot *read* anything which lies distinctly outside our life experience. To be sure, we may feel, experience, understand new particulars, but that is possible because the
basis for such learning already exists within us. In such cases, the
book merely apprises us of what we are already but did not quite
recall. Emerson's adherence to this epistemological principle is
what justifies Harold Bloom to remark that in Emerson's writings
"there is no author but ourselves; . . . a strong reading indeed is
the only text." This self-reflexivity is what Bloom means by
gnosis. For him it is distinctive of the Emersonian vision, to such
a degree that "a discourse upon Emerson's Gnosis, to be Emersonian rather than literary historical, itself must be Gnosis, or
part of a Gnosis. It must speak of a knowing in which the knower
himself is known, a reading in which he is read."[4]
The troubling corollary of this principle is that the reading
experience becomes sharply divergent. The same book will never
mean the same thing to two different people. Indeed, as Emerson
remarked, "Cousin is a thousand books to a thousand persons."
Readerly consensus, in this view, is suspect, if not precluded altogether. What then becomes of the whole project of criticism and
interpretation? The answer, of course, is that it becomes another
phase of writing. Reading loses its distinct status as commentary
and becomes an exercise in self-revelation. This is an implication
which seems to have bothered Emerson hardly at all. He never
lost much love on "biographies, histories, and criticism" anyway.

It was he, after all, who famously insisted that "one must be an inventor to read well." There is "creative reading, as well as creative writing"; indeed we might go so far as to say that creative reading is a kind of creative writing (CW, I, 58). If the reader is good enough, the pages of the text become luminous and disappear; the reader then is left alone in dialogue with himself.

Emerson's hermeneutical epistemology and its corollary would degenerate into mystical subjectivism were it not for his idea of a developmental scale or hierarchy of interpretation, and his constraining idea of its highest level. Variations of interpretation to a text bear some correspondence to, in fact are the reflections of, different levels of human development. So an illiterate man sees only black marks on a page, a child recognizes words he has come to know, and a sage sees secrets to be revealed. At each reading level, the meaning of the text depends on the state of consciousness of the reader, and on nothing else. At the highest rungs of this ladder of interpretation, the reader recovers the fuller meaning of what the writer specifically intended. But even that recognition does not place a cap on the reader's interpretation, since if the reading is vigorous enough, the page becomes as wide as the world (CW, I, 58). The reader, that is, may wind up comprehending the author to such an extent that he sees way beyond the borders of the author's conscious intention. Nevertheless, this old intentional model of interpretation, while it proves a fallacy in Emerson's conception of reading, still provides him with a principle of correspondence which prevents his hermeneutics from turning into unqualified subjective chaos. In the case of literary texts, Emerson simply did not mind extravagant interpretations, as his tutee Thoreau well knew. But in religious texts, and in all inspired literature, such extravagance was governed by an overarching critical principle: "Every scripture is to be interpreted by the same spirit which gave it forth." This, says Emerson, "is the fundamental law of criticism" (CW, I, 23).

Coming as it does at the end of the "Language" section of *Nature*, this announcement of George Fox's exegetical guideline suggests its relevance also to our reading of *Nature*. It is Emerson's formulation of the cutting edge which separates the wheat from the chaff. We may read *Nature* extravagantly (there is hardly any other way to read it), but that does not necessarily mean we are reading it rightly. And whether we do or not does not depend on the literacy as much as the "spirit" of the reader. The readers for whom *Nature* has been waiting are the ones who read from the same source that *Nature* was written from. These are few and far between; they are *Nature*'s elect. Their reading is still extravagant, but it is an extravagance that is guided by the same vision as the author's. This may seem to land us back in the genetic fallacy or some more conventional correspondence idea of interpretation, but this is not what Emerson means. He does not want readers to return to the understandings and intentions of the author. The particulars are without significance. What is significant is not so much the particular interpretation as the spirit, the vision, in which such interpretation is realized.

A clue to this may be found in the lecture on English literature, cited above, which Emerson delivered in 1835. "A good reader," we remember, "needs the high qualities of a good writer. . . . The pupil must conspire with the Teachers. It needs Shakspear, it needs Bacon, to read Shakspear and Bacon in the best manner." For Emerson the word *conspire* seems to connote more than simply a breathing together. As we saw in our discussion of the epiphany in "Beauty," Emerson loads this word with the tendencies of his spiraling, centrifugal vision. Even in the passage above there is perhaps a certain word play—it is the "pupil" after all which conspires with the teachers. In "Beauty" conspiration is clearly a movement of vision: "From the earth, as a shore, I look out into that silent sea. I seem to partake its rapid transformations: the active enchantment reaches my dust, and I dilate and conspire with the morning wind" (CW, I, 13). What the reader realizes here is not, therefore, the substance of the writer's views but how they come about. So in the books of great writers, it is not the reading matter that is significant but the reading process. "There is a right way of reading," Emerson warned, and indicated that it necessarily involved "periods of solitude, inquest and self-recovery" (CW, I, 57).

Here then is another formulation of Emerson's conception of easting. It is the most that should be gained from another person's book and the best that can be. His own book was conceived, its rhetoric inspired and deployed, to instigate this process of expression and reflection in the consciousness of his reader. It was the produce and the tendency of his revelation. Right reading was for Emerson a species of meditation. The printed page functioned merely as commentary—to be consulted only when the illuminated characters of the self had become corrupt or unintelligible. To justify itself reading must be a perpetual expression of easting. The procession of symbols on the printed page must be renounced periodically in deference to the edicts of the self. Reading was a continual effort of reorientation—a circle which, involving the alien word, curved continuously back to its interior point of origin. Whenever a day comes when the commentary no longer seems germane, when it seems redundant, wrong, or out of date, that is the signal to put the book down. Then the reading will be equal to the writing.[5]

This is the kind of reader that Emerson envisioned for his own book. At the start of "Prospects" he pauses for a moment to consider what such an ideal reader ought to be like. The text he tests him on is the ideal text—the Book of Nature. "The best read naturalist," he writes, "who lends an entire and devout attention to truth, will see that there remains much to learn of his relation to the world." Whether in the text of the world or some lowlier book, the basic thing to be learned is the same: what is the relation of the reader to the text? Every reading begins in alienation and moves toward some degree of reconciliation. What needs to be overcome is this original division between the book and its reader. But this can never happen, insists Emerson, "by any addition or subtraction or other comparison of known quantities." Something more radical is necessary to bridge this gulf than the adjustments and analysis of the discursive understanding. In the end nothing will satisfy the reader until the interpretation turns back on the self. Final knowledge, whether of the relation of the individual and the world or the reader and the text, will only be "arrived at by untaught sallies of the spirit, by a continual self-recovery, and by entire humility" (CW, I, 39). These are the mechanics of right reading. It is periodic: aggressive sallies follow hard on the heels of self-emptying; the creation of meaning, the creation of the text, follows the abandonment of meaning, the renunciation of the text. In such a strong reading the separation between the text and the reader is overcome when the text becomes the creation of the reader.

In all this discussion of the reader in *Nature* or, as Stanley Fish might put it, *Nature* in the reader, the question arises as to whether we are speaking in terms of fact or fiction. Emerson, as we have seen, envisioned an elect or ideal readership; so did Whitman and Thoreau. But in what sense do such readers exist? Iser maintains that the ideal reader, while providing a useful construct, is nevertheless "a purely fictional being."[6] Kermode doubts the very possibility of an elect reader—the insider—since in the final analysis all readers are outsiders. It is the nature of texts to exclude. The very conception of a textual inner sanctum is for him a kind of myth deriving from the nature of the text itself.[7] It may well be that the wise reader conceived by Emerson was also in the long run a kind of myth, but my discussion of Emerson's revelation suggests that there is some reason for grounding his mythic-apocalyptic reader in flesh and blood also.

The main objection leveled at the existence of the ideal reader, whether Emerson's or someone else's, is that in actual reading experience the implicit meanings of a text will always far exceed the significance perceived by any particular reader. No single reading or reader can ever exhaust the nearly infinite suggestive potential of any complex literary or religious text. The possibility of radical divergence of response among readers to any given text is what troubles many traditionally minded critics about any approach to interpretation which insists on placing the reader at the center of the critical process. Rampant subjectivity, lack of consensus, chaos seem the inevitable results. For the vast majority of texts, such sanctioning, even glorification, of subjective response seems unworkable if not perverse. Yet for a limited category of texts, ambitious texts, perhaps mostly religious texts, such an approach to criticism seems not only appropriate but specifically dictated by evidence of authorial intention and rhetorical strategy. *Nature* is one such text. Emerson, as we have seen, was not at all uncomfortable with the prospect of individual appropriation of his book. In fact, he applauded and colluded with it. But, in the case of *Nature,* such sanction did not lead necessarily to uncontainable divergence of response. To be sure, *Nature*'s readers may

always and legitimately re-create the text differently, but in order to do so completely they must do so in the same way. The ideal
or elect reader in *Nature* is not the reader who fathoms all its
potential meanings; he is the reader who conceives *Nature* as it
was conceived in the beginning. And in order for this to happen
fully and authentically, the reader must participate in the apocalyptic movement of destruction and creation which the book is
about.

The second objection to the ideal reader idea is that the real
existence of such a reader would render the text superfluous,
since if he already shares the full significance of the text there is
no need for him or her to read it. In the case of *Nature* specifically,
the ideal reader would already be naturally disposed to the movements of easting and so would not find anything new in *Nature*'s
gaps and spirals. For such a reader the page would already be a
spontaneous transparency. This objection is compelling. For Emerson, the elect reader he sought was indeed a myth. But by this I
do not mean to say that the mythical reader was unreal: I think
Emerson believed such readers existed. The misrepresentation
here is not that they existed but that they were the ones he was
writing for. Nature, after all, is only efficacious for those readers
for whom easting is not already habitual. The vision of the ideal
reader is the goal of our reading; the path involves "untaught
sallies," "continual self-recovery," and much "humility." For most
of us, reading Emerson involves purification and labor, a process
which, if we are attentive, results in moments of transparency. It
is reading which changes us, gives us room to breathe and stretch
to our fuller dimensions. *Nature* is not the vision itself, it is the
practicing of vision, and the reader is the practitioner.

In the penultimate stage of the composition of *Nature,* Emerson,
we may remember, expressed concern about the last remaining
"crack" in his book. Digging into the journals and letters, and
scrutinizing the apparent seams of *Nature,* scholars have been
eager to identify precisely that crack. Undoubtedly, Emerson had a
particular link of his argument in mind, and undoubtedly it had
something to do with the transition between nature and spirit. But
perhaps it might prove even more revealing of *Nature*'s design if
we were not so hasty in restricting its exact location. The crack is,

in one form or another, *the* condition which *Nature* strives to over-come. It is not only a crack between chapters in a book; it is the crack between world and spirit, the reader and the text, the sign and its significance, the reader and the self. The world we start with is fractured and fissured all over. It is the task of *Nature* to close all these gaps. It does not do so philosophically, at least not primarily. Rather, it relies on a host of strategies, all literary and rhetorical. It reworks types and extends symbols; it leans on myth and allegory; it concentrates in aphorisms and conspires in the spaces between them. In all this the point is to bring about a re-union and marriage between the intelligence that wrote the book and the one that reads it. The best books, said Emerson, impress upon us the conviction "that one nature wrote and the same reads" (CW, I, 57). When lecturing on English literature, Emerson made the same point more vividly:

> I know few more agreeable offices in the opportunities of common life than to introduce a good mind to the writings of a kindred intelligence. It must be our main object to consummate this marriage between the mind of the scholar and the mind of the author. Literature resembles religion in many respects and their fortunes have been commonly related. It must be possessed by the man or it is naught. (EL, I, 211)

Marriage is a governing theme in Emerson's *Nature,* as it was in the apocalyptic writings that he drew upon for his imaginative design. In the Book of Revelation, the consummation of marriage came after the consummation of the world; in *Nature* the consum-mation of marriage results in the consummation of the world and then the vision of the new heaven and earth. This can happen only because the minds in union are not two minds at all, but one mind. "It is God in you," wrote Emerson earlier, "that responds to God without or affirms his own words trembling on the lips of another" (JMN, III, 302). In its highest expressions this marriage dissolves the cracks because it dissolves the world. In this vision there is no sense of self and other, only being. This is the way Emerson understood the vision of Saint John of Patmos, and this is the way he conceived his purpose in *Nature*. "Touch the deep heart and all these listless stingy beefeating bystanders will see the dignity of a sentiment, will say This is good and all I have I will give for that. Excite the soul, and the weather and the town and your condition in the world all disappear, the world itself loses its solidity, nothing remains but the soul and the Divine Presence in which it lives" (JMN, IV, 383).

For Emerson literature not only resembled religion, it continued its work. It must be "possessed" by the reader, internalized, or it is of no value. There is no disjunction between the apocalypse of Saint John and the one in *Nature*. It is the same project, only revised to make it effective. The work of art dissolves the old world to make way for the new. It brings the reader back to the point of freshness just before the dawn of the new heaven and earth. This was the purpose of art for Emerson. "Art," he wrote, "should exhilarate, and throw down the walls of circumstance on every side, awakening in the beholder the same sense of universal relation and power which the work evinced in the artist, and its highest effect is to make new artists" (CW, II, 216). The revelation Emerson saw was old, yet continuous. It did not end with one epoch or one canon, but had to be realized again by each new reader with each new reading. In the Bible it was the prophet who saw the new heaven and the new earth; in nineteenth-century New England this vision was passing to the poet. The functions were the same, with one important revision: where it had been the prophet's responsibility to announce the apocalypse, it was the poet's role to inaugurate its recapitulation.

Notes

Introduction

1. *The Christian Examiner,* 21 January 1837, pp. 371–76. Anthologized in Perry Miller, ed., *The Transcendentalists: An Anthology* (Cambridge: Harvard University Press, 1950), pp. 173–76; also available in Merton M. Sealts, Jr., and Alfred R. Ferguson, eds., *Emerson's "Nature": Origin, Growth, Meaning,* 2nd ed. (Carbondale and Edwardsville: Southern Illinois University Press, 1969), pp. 81–88.

2. B. L. Packer, *Emerson's Fall: A New Interpretation of the Major Essays* (New York: Continuum, 1982), p. 23.

3. Oliver Wendell Holmes, *Ralph Waldo Emerson,* American Men of Letters Series (Boston and New York: Houghton and Mifflin Company, 1884), p. 93.

4. Harold Bloom, *Agon: Towards a Theory of Revisionism* (New York: Oxford University Press, 1982), p. 156.

5. Packer, *Emerson's Fall,* p. 81; Maurice Gonnaud, "Nature, Apocalypse or Experiment," in *Vistas of a Continent: Concepts of Nature in America,* ed. T. A. Riese (Heidelberg, 1979), p. 125.

6. Joel Porte, *Representative Man: Ralph Waldo Emerson in His Time* (New York: Oxford University Press, 1979), pp. 64–86.

7. Edwin Gittleman, *Jones Very: The Effective Years, 1833–1840* (New York and London: Columbia University Press, 1976), pp. 122–30. Very's copy of *Nature* is included in the Parkman Dexter Howe Collection of the University of Florida Library. CEC, 157.

8. Holmes, *Emerson,* p. 103.

Chapter 1

1. For a ready overview of the central role of the Bible in American history, see Nathan O. Hatch and Mark A. Noll, eds., *The Bible in America: Essays in Cultural History* (New York: Oxford University Press, 1982).

2. Cf. also JMN, V, 140: "C. [Charles] asks if I were condemned to solitude and one book—which would I choose? We agreed that Milton would have no claims, and that the Bible must be preferred to Shakspear, because the last, one could better supply himself. The first has a higher strain."

3. For a survey of Emerson's explicit use of the Bible, see Harriet Rogers Zink, "Emerson's Use of the Bible," *University of Nebraska Studies in Language, Literature, and Criticism,* no. 14 (Lincoln, 1935).

4. For a helpful discussion of the higher criticism, see Hans W. Frei's *The Eclipse of Biblical Narrative: A Study in Eighteenth and Nineteenth Century Hermeneutics* (New Haven: Yale University Press, 1974). See also Jerry Wayne Brown, *The Rise of Biblical Criticism in America, 1800–1870: The New England Scholars* (Middletown, Conn.: Wesleyan University Press, 1969); and Barbara Packer, "Origin and Authority: Emerson and the Higher Criticism," in *Reconstructing American Literary History,* ed. Sacvan Bercovitch (Cambridge and London: Harvard University Press, 1986).

5. Ralph L. Rusk, *The Life of Ralph Waldo Emerson* (New York: Columbia University Press, 1949), pp. 76–79.

6. Rusk, *Emerson,* p. 103.

7. Stephen E. Whicher, *Freedom and Fate: An Inner Life of Ralph Waldo Emerson* (Philadelphia: University of Pennsylvania Press, 1953).

8. Rusk, *Emerson,* p. 105.

9. Cf. JMN, V, 186, 466–67; W, VII, 208.

10. Jonathan Edwards, *Images and Shadows of Divine Things by Jonathan Edwards,* ed. Perry Miller (New Haven: Yale University Press, 1948).

11. For a glimpse of Mary Moody Emerson's own raptures in nature and her debt to Edwards in this respect, see Phyllis Cole, "The Advantage of Loneliness: Mary Moody Emerson's Almanacks, 1802–1855," in *Emerson: Prospect and Retrospect,* ed. Joel Porte, Harvard English Studies 10 (Cambridge: Harvard University Press, 1982), p. 16.

12. See Ernst Robert Curtius, *European Literature and the Latin Middle Ages,* trans. Willard R. Trask (Princeton: Princeton University Press, 1953), pp. 319–26.

13. *Religio Medici* (1643), pt. 1, ch. 15; quoted in Curtius, p. 323.

14. See, for example, *Paradise Lost,* 8.66–68.

15. Porte, *Representative Man,* pp. 70–71.

16. Sampson Reed, *Observations on the Growth of the Mind* (Boston: Cummings and Hilliard, 1826), pp. 24–25.

17. Guillaume Oegger, *The True Messiah; or, The Old and New Testaments Examined According to the Principles of the Language of Nature* (Boston: Peabody, 1842).

18. Thomas Carlyle, *Sartor Resartus: The Life and Opinions of Herr Teufelsdröckh,* vol. 1 of *The Works of Thomas Carlyle* (New York: AMS Press, 1969), p. 205.

19. Running parallel to this main tradition, it should be noted, is a more heterodox one which is descended from certain Gnostic and neo-Platonic conceptions of nature as an irretrievably fallen order. This tradition is best represented by Boehme—with whose teachings Emerson and Coleridge were familiar—and Blake. It rejected any sanguine belief in the correspondence of human and natural orders, and viewed the physical world with suspicion—an attitude to which, as we shall see, Emerson was also no stranger. See CW, I, 35: "Some theosophists have arrived at a certain hostility and indignation towards matter, as the Manichean and Plotinus."

20. Northrop Frye, *The Great Code: The Bible and Literature* (New York and London: Harcourt Brace Jovanovich, 1982), p. 78.

21. Edwards, *Images or Shadows of Divine Things.* See Mason I. Lowance, Jr., *The Language of Canaan: Metaphor and Symbol in New England from the Puritans to the Transcendentalists* (Cambridge: Harvard University Press, 1980), pp. 196ff.; and Barbara Kiefer Lewalski, *Protestant Poetics and the Seventeenth-Century Religious Lyric* (Princeton: Princeton University Press, 1979), pp. 139–40.

22. On the wider regional and historical context of Emerson's project, see Lawrence Buell's chapter "Literary Scripturism" in his *New England Literary Culture: From Revolution Through Renaissance* (Cambridge and London: Cambridge University Press, 1986), pp. 166–90.

23. F. O. Matthiessen, *American Renaissance: Art and Expression in the Age of Emerson and Whitman* (New York: Oxford University Press, 1941), p. 23.

24. Warner Berthoff, " 'Building Discourse': The Genesis of Emerson's *Nature,*" in *Fictions and Events: Essays in Criticism and Literary History* (New York: E. P. Dutton & Co., 1971).

25. Lawrence Buell, *Literary Transcendentalism: Style and Vision in the American Renaissance* (Ithaca: Cornell University Press, 1973), p. 135.

26. Buell, *Literary Transcendentalism,* pp. 139ff.

27. Coleridge's Scripture, like Emerson's *Nature,* constituted a "system of symbols, harmonious in themselves, and cosubstantial with the truths, of which they are the conductors." Samuel Taylor Coleridge, *Lay*

Sermons, ed. R. J. White, in *The Collected Works of Samuel Taylor Coleridge* (Princeton: Princeton University Press, 1972), pp. 28–30.

28. For the best survey of the enormous impact of "Revelation" on Western life and literature, see C. A. Patrides and Joseph Wittreich, eds., *The Apocalypse in English Renaissance Thought and Literature* (Ithaca: Cornell University Press, 1984).

29. M. H. Abrams, *Natural Supernaturalism: Tradition and Revolution in Romantic Literature* (New York: Norton, 1971), p. 41.

30. As Abrams notes, there is some disagreement among biblical commentators as to where, in fact, this new paradise is located, in heaven or on earth. Milton dismisses the question as of little account in *The Christian Doctrine,* I, xxxiii. See Abrams, pp. 41–42.

31. Cf. Is. 61.10; Hos. 2.16–23; Mt. 25.1; Jn. 3.29; 2 Cor. 11.1–2.

32. All quoted from Abrams, *Natural Supernaturalism,* pp. 27–31.

33. Holmes, *Emerson,* p. 92.

34. Porte, *Representative Man,* pp. 72–73; EL, II, 273.

35. See also EL, I, 24.

36. For an illuminating parallel to Emerson's marriage allegory, note the so-called Orc cycle as it is represented, for example, in Blake's "The Mental Traveler," in *The Poetry and Prose of William Blake,* ed. David V. Erdman, with commentary by Harold Bloom (Garden City, N.Y.: Doubleday and Company, 1970), pp. 475–77. See also Northrop Frye's commentary in *Fearful Symmetry: A Study of William Blake* (Princeton: Princeton University Press, 1947), pp. 225ff.

37. For another example of this metaphorical association between wool and snow among biblical writers, see Ps. 147.16.

Chapter 2

1. Packer, *Emerson's Fall,* pp. 72–84.

2. Whicher, *Freedom and Fate,* p. 57; Sherman Paul, *Emerson's Angle of Vision: Man and Nature in American Experience* (Cambridge: Harvard University Press, 1952), pp. 34–36. Recognition of the centrality in Emerson's writings of this alternating movement between freedom and fate continues to open new critical perspectives, as Julie Ellison's recent study on Emerson's style exemplifies. See Julie Ellison, *Emerson's Romantic Style* (Princeton: Princeton University Press, 1984).

3. Samuel Taylor Coleridge, *The Friend* (1818), ed. Barbara E. Rooke, 2 vols., in *The Collected Works of Samuel Taylor Coleridge* (Princeton: Princeton University Press, 1969), vol. I, p. 479; quoted in Packer, *Emerson's Fall,* p. 45.

4. Samuel Taylor Coleridge, *Biographia Literaria* (1817), ed. James Engell and W. Jackson Bate, 2 vols., in *The Collected Works of Samuel*

Taylor Coleridge (Princeton: Princeton University Press, 1983), vol. I, p. 286.

5. Coleridge, *Biographia Literaria,* vol. II, p. 297.

6. See also CW, II, 72.

7. Rusk, *Emerson,* p. 111.

8. It is possible to multiply these instances. For another striking early example, see JMN, II, 45, which begins: "The sublimest scene which ever opened on the thought of man, is the Judgement of the World, in the partial representations of the sacred writers."

9. I am indebted to Phyllis Cole, who has kindly helped to support and clarify my intuitions about the importance of this relationship. See Cole, "The Advantage of Loneliness."

10. Whicher, *Freedom and Fate,* p. 8.

11. In a letter of 1824 which Emerson transcribed into his journal, Mary seems to voice some regret at the boosterism she showed to her young nephews. Here she blames "the atmosphere of theology," her own "speculation," and above all "the sore of human nature" for any harm her early permissiveness may have caused (J, II, 31).

12. Rusk, *Emerson,* p. 230.

13. Cf. also JMN, IV, 46: "The true statement concerning retribution, is, that human nature is self retributive. Every moment is a judgment day, because, every act puts the agent in a new condition."

14. In modern theology this kenotic Christology received its first systematic treatment in mid-nineteenth-century Germany, where it flourished for a time, starting with the publication in 1845 of Thomasius's *Beiträge zur Kirchlichen Christologie.* From Germany it migrated at the end of the century to England, where it has enjoyed a considerable vogue among English theologians and clerics. See John MacQuarrie, "Kenoticism Reconsidered," *Theology,* vol. 77, no. 654 (March 1974); Graham James, "The Enduring Appeal of Kenotic Christology," *Theology,* vol. 86, no. 709 (January 1983).

15. Whicher, *Freedom and Fate,* p. 28.

16. J, II, 497–50. On Emerson and the Quakers, see F. B. Tolles, "Emerson and Quakerism," *American Literature,* vol. 10 (1938), 142–65; M. C. Turpie, "A Quaker Source for Emerson's Sermon on the Lord's Supper," *New England Quarterly,* vol. 17 (1944), 95–101.

17. Cf. EL, II, 292–93.

18. For the Quaker, in contrast, for example, to the Methodist, conversion is not a precipitous event but a gradual process of inner tuning. The same was true for Emerson, since when "the Kingdom of man over nature" comes, it does so, we may remember, "gradually" (CW, I, 45). For a useful outline of the stages of Quaker regeneration, see Howard H. Brinton, *Quaker Journals: Varieties of Religious Experience Among Friends* (Wallingford, Pa.: Pendle Hill Publications, 1972).

19. Whicher, *Freedom and Fate,* pp. 13–26; see also Packer, *Emerson's Fall,* pp. 34–41.

20. Among twentieth-century readers and social commentators, Emerson has enjoyed a checkered reputation at best. Much recent debate in the popular and academic press has centered on the legacy of his famous Self-reliance; see, for example, the references to Emerson and Self-reliance in Robert N. Bellah et al., *Habits of the Heart: Individualism and Commitment in American Life* (Berkeley and Los Angeles: University of California Press, 1985). Some, it seems, would have us believe that Emerson is to blame for such defects in our national character as narcissism and the breakdown of community. It is true of course that from the beginning of his public career Emerson has been the victim of caricature and one-sided reading. Whatever "Self-reliance" may have become in the minds and hearts of later Americans, it was not in its original conception narcissistic or indeed opposed to community. On the contrary, Emerson by his nature detested narcissism; in fact, one of the main implications of our recognition that the roots of Self-reliance lie in a piety of charity and self-denial is that Emerson could only have dismissed such readings in patient disbelief.

21. In a journal entry on humility which Emerson made in the summer of 1830, he paraphrased Matthew 23.12 this way: "He that humbleth himself shall be exalted because he that humbleth himself—it is a sign that he is exalting his idea of the power of his own nature and of course perceives the mediocrity of his own attainments; and is exalting his view of God" (JMN, III, 190).

22. "Know Thyself." JMN, III, 290–95. See also Kenneth Walter Cameron, *Emerson the Essayist,* vol. 1 (Raleigh, N.C.: Thistle Press, 1945), pp. 169–80; and Whicher, *Freedom and Fate,* pp. 23–26.

23. Cf. JMN, IV, 47–48, 52, 58, 84, 87, etc.

24. Carlyle, *Sartor Resartus,* pp. 148–49.

25. John Albee, *Remembrances of Emerson* (New York: Robert G. Cooke, 1901), p. 58; quoted in John McAleer, *Ralph Waldo Emerson: Days of Encounter* (Boston: Little, Brown, 1984), p. 231.

26. Frye, *The Great Code,* p. 138.

27. See Abrams, *Natural Supernaturalism,* pp. 46–56.

28. James M. Cox, "R. W. Emerson: The Circles of the Eye," in *Emerson: Prophecy, Metamorphosis, and Influence,* ed. David Levin (New York: Columbia University Press, 1975), pp. 71–72; Kenneth Burke, "I, Eye, Aye—Emerson's Early Essay 'Nature': Thoughts on the Machinery of Transcendence," in *Transcendentalism and Its Legacy,* ed. Myron Simon and Thornton H. Parsons (Ann Arbor: University of Michigan Press, 1966), p. 21; Packer, *Emerson's Fall,* pp. 48–57.

29. Biblical sanction for this doctrine can be found in Rom. 4.17 and Heb. 11.3.

30. See, for example, Karl Barth, *The Doctrine of Creation,* in *Church*

Dogmatics, authorized English translation, vol. 3, 1 (Edinburgh: T. and T. Clark, 1958), pp. 3–41.

Chapter 3

1. See, for example, 1 Cor. 15.44 in "Language" (CW, I, 19); 2 Cor. 1.17 in "Discipline" (CW, I, 24); 2 Cor. 4.18 in "Idealism" (CW, I, 35).
2. Northrop Frye, *Fables of Identity: Studies in Poetic Mythology* (New York and London: Harcourt Brace Jovanovich, 1963), p. 36.
3. See Porte, *Representative Man,* pp. viff. On Emerson's rhetorical strategy in "Circles," see Jack Null, "Strategies of Imagery in 'Circles,' " *Emerson Society Quarterly,* vol. 18, no. 4, pp. 265–70; Albert H. Tricomi, "The Rhetoric of Aspiring Circularity in Emerson's 'Circles,' " ibid., pp. 271–83; David M. Wyatt, "Spelling Time: The Reader in Emerson's 'Circles,' " *American Literature,* vol. 48, no. 2 (1976), 140–51.
4. For the context and background of this emendation, see Richard Lee Francis, "Completing the Sphere: Emerson's Revisions of the Mottoes of *Nature,*" in *Studies in the American Renaissance,* ed. Joel Myerson (Boston: Twayne Publishers, 1979), pp. 231–37.
5. CW, I, 12, 17, 26, 37.
6. Kenneth Walter Cameron, *Emerson the Essayist,* vol. 1 (Raleigh, N.C.: Thistle Press, 1945), pp. 110–11; Rusk, *Emerson,* p. 143.
7. Coleridge, *The Friend,* vol. I, p. 457.
8. See also JMN, V, 163, and Sealts and Ferguson, *Emerson's "Nature,"* pp. 60, 178, 205 n. 5.
9. Cf. Ellison, *Emerson's Romantic Style,* pp. 87–88.
10. For the purposes of my interpretation here, I have thought it best to work with the 1836 text. Where a revision from the 1849 edition proves illuminating, I have provided it.
11. R. A. Yoder, *Emerson and the Orphic Poet in America* (Berkeley: University of California Press, 1978), p. 93.
12. See, for example, JMN, II, 153, 170.
13. On the origin of this locution, see Porte, *Representative Man,* p. 50.
14. Joel Porte suggests that Emerson may have been in pursuit of "a process of self-recovery—a way of reanimating and reorienting the self—" as early as his first trip to Europe in 1833. Its roots, I believe, go back even further than that (Porte, *Representative Man,* p. 50).
15. Paul, *Emerson's Angle of Vision,* p. 85.
16. Coleridge, *Biographia Literaria,* vol. I, p. 297.
17. Yet it ought to be noted that this lofty conception of the inspired artist had something of the mythic about it. Emerson himself was painstaking in his compositions and well aware that even enthusiasm had its limits, as is evidenced by his memorably ironic response to some of Jones Very's divinely dictated inspirations: "Cannot the spirit parse and spell?"

18. There have been numerous discussions of Emerson's preoccupation with vision. Besides Sherman Paul, compare Burke, "I, Eye, Aye—Emerson's Early Essay 'Nature,' " in *Transcendentalism and Its Legacy,* ed. Myron Simon and Thornton H. Parsons (Ann Arbor: University of Michigan Press, 1966), pp. 3–24; Tony Tanner, *The Reign of Wonder* (New York: Harper, 1967), ch. 2, "Emerson: The Unconquered Eye and the Enchanted Circle."

19. Whicher, *Freedom and Fate, p. 132.*

20. Jonathan Bishop, *Emerson on the Soul* (Cambridge: Harvard University Press, 1964), p. 15.

21. Cf. Victor Turner, "Myth and Symbol," in *International Encyclopedia of the Social Sciences* [1968], ed. D. L. Sills, vol. 10, pp. 576–82.

22. When Jane Carlyle summarized her first impressions of Emerson after his visit to Craigenputtock in 1833, she wrote: "I should never forget the Visitor, who years ago in the Desart descended on us, out of the clouds, as it were, and made one day there look like enchantment for us, and left me weeping that it was only *one* day" (CEC, 201). See also Rusk, *Emerson,* p. 195.

23. Bishop, *Emerson on the Soul,* p. 233 n. 14; Sealts and Ferguson, *Emerson's "Nature,"* p. 182 n. 9.

24. For the most authoritative and influential exposition of this important idea, see Matthiessen, *American Renaissance,* pp. 133–75. Also cf. Vivian C. Hopkins, *Spires of Form: A Study of Emerson's Aesthetic Theory* (Cambridge: Harvard University Press, 1951).

25. Indeed, if Harold Bloom is right, such antagonism is true of all revisionism. See Bloom, *Agon.*

Chapter 4

1. Sealts and Ferguson, *Emerson's "Nature,"* pp. 65–66.

2. Miller, *The Transcendentalists,* p. 174.

3. In 1835 Emerson explicitly endorsed Aristotle's view of the essential function of literature and argued that "the poem was a transcript of nature as much as a mariner's chart is of the coast," but there is a certain dissembling in such claims, as my discussion of the real origins of *Nature* has sought to show. EL, I, 215. For more familiar declarations of such organicism, see also "The Poet" (CW, III, 5–6, 14–15, etc.).

4. See Berthoff, *Fictions and Events,* pp. 191ff.

5. Also CW, I, 19, 40.

6. William Haller, *The Rise of Puritanism; or The Way to The New Jerusalem as Set Forth in Pulpit and Press from Thomas Cartwright to John Lilburne and John Milton, 1570–1643* (New York: Columbia University Press, 1938), pp. 134ff. See also Lawrence Buell, "The Unitarian

Movement and the Art of Preaching in 19th Century America," *American Quarterly,* vol. 24 (1972).

7. The phrase is Said's. See Edward W. Said, *Beginnings: Intention and Method* (Baltimore: Johns Hopkins University Press, 1975), p. 262; quoted in Ellison, *Emerson's Romantic Style,* p. 160.

8. Ellison, *Emerson's Romantic Style,* pp. 168ff.

9. CW, I, 27, 15–16, 20, 22, 25–28, 35–36.

10. Berthoff, *Fictions and Events,* p. 212.

11. Buell, *Literary Transcendentalism,* pp. 166–87.

12. Cf. CW, I, 12, 13, 14, 17, 23, 31, 43, 44.

13. David Porter, *Emerson and Literary Change* (Cambridge: Harvard University Press, 1978), p. 207.

14. Matthiessen, *American Renaissance,* pp. 64–65.

15. Frye, *The Great Code,* pp. 212–13.

16. Matthiessen, *American Renaissance,* p. 65.

17. S. T. Coleridge, *Aids to Reflection, in The Formation of a Manly Character on the several grounds of Prudence, Morality, and Religion,* ed. James Marsh (Burlington, Vt., 1829), p. 11; note, pp. 257–58.

18. Susanne K. Langer, *Philosophy in a New Key: A Study in the Symbolism of Reason, Rite, and Art* (Cambridge: Harvard University Press, 1942), p. 97.

19. For a useful survey of this growing body of criticism, see Jane P. Tompkins, ed., *Reader Response Criticism: From Formalism to Post-Structuralism* (Baltimore: Johns Hopkins University Press, 1980).

20. Coleridge, *Lay Sermons,* p. 30.

21. Langer, *Philosophy in a New Key,* p. 97.

22. Frank Kermode, *The Sense of an Ending: Studies in the Theory of Fiction* (New York: Oxford University Press, 1966), p. 47. Kermode derives the above distinction from various modern theologians, especially Oscar Cullman in *Christ and Time* (Philadelphia: Westminster Press, 1950), and John Marsh, *The Fullness of Time* (New York: Harper and Brothers, 1952).

23. Carlyle, *Sartor Resartus,* pp. 57, 41.

24. Cf. Emerson's remarks on Bacon's lack of system: "All his work lies along the ground, a vast unfinished city" (EL, I, 335). While Emerson's writings are not quite so miscellaneous as Bacon's, there are nevertheless significant parallels here. Cf. Ellison, *Emerson's Romantic Style,* pp. 157ff.

25. Wolfgang Iser, *The Act of Reading: A Theory of Aesthetic Response* (Baltimore: Johns Hopkins University Press, 1978), pp. 24, 166ff.

26. See Erich Auerbach, *Mimesis: The Representation of Reality in Western Literature,* trans. Willard R. Trask (Princeton: Princeton University Press, 1953).

27. Amos Bronson Alcott, *Ralph Waldo Emerson; Philosopher and*

Seer: An Estimate of His Character and Genius, 2nd ed. (Boston: Cupples and Hurd, 1888), p. 35; quoted in Ellison, *Emerson's Romantic Style,* pp. 170–71.

28. JMN, III, 26. Cited in Ellison, *Emerson's Romantic Style,* p. 3.

29. Perry Miller, *The American Transcendentalists: Their Prose and Poetry* (Garden City, N.Y.: Doubleday, 1957), p. 96.

30. See also Packer, *Emerson's Fall.*

31. While Emerson was journeying up the Nile, Mrs. Helen Bell, one of his townswomen, was said to have been asked: "What do you think the Sphinx said to Mr. Emerson?" "Why," she replied, "the Sphinx probably said to him 'your another'!" Quoted in Packer, *Emerson's Fall,* p. 23.

32. See Merton M. Sealts, Jr., "Emerson as Teacher," in *Emerson Centenary Essays,* ed. Joel Myerson (Carbondale: Southern Illinois University Press, 1982), pp. 180–90.

Chapter 5

1. For perhaps the most influential formulations of this mode of exegesis, see Augustine, *De Doctrina Christiana,* II.10, III.27; Aquinas, *Summa Theologica,* I, Q. 1, Art. 10. A survey of traditional forms of interpretations is provided in Robert M. Grant, with David Tracy, *A Short History of Biblical Interpretation,* 2nd ed., rev. (Philadelphia: Fortress Press, 1971).

2. Frank Kermode, *The Genesis of Secrecy: On the Interpretation of Narrative* (Cambridge: Harvard University Press, 1979).

3. A near antecedent to Emerson's conception of hermeneutical election may be found in much seventeenth-century Puritan exegesis, which, in reaction to what was seen as licentious subjectivity in the Catholic multileveled interpretation, imposed the stricture that the Bible could be truly understood only by a regenerate believer. While this precondition was meant by its sponsors to preclude divergent interpretations of Scripture, its result ironically was to pave the way for them. On the background and irony of this requirement, see Sacvan Bercovitch, *The Puritan Origins of the American Self* (New Haven and London: Yale University Press, 1975), pp. 110ff.

4. Bloom, *Agon,* p. 170.

5. In what is still one of the most perceptive and well-documented accounts of the role of the reader in Emerson's writings, Vivian Hopkins underscores the intended "mystical" dimension in the reader's response. See Vivian C. Hopkins, *Spires of Form: A Study of Emerson's Aesthetic Theory* (Cambridge: Harvard University Press, 1951), ch. 3.

6. Iser, *The Act of Reading,* p. 29.

7. Kermode, *The Genesis of Secrecy.*

Index